Enjoy!
Merry Christmas
I Love You,
Gina

THE INWARD JOURNEY

The
INWARD JOURNEY

by

HOWARD THURMAN

Friends United Press

Richmond, Indiana

Grateful acknowledgment is made to Harcourt, Brace & World, Inc., and to Faber and Faber, Ltd., for permission to quote "The Hollow Men" in *Collected Poems 1909-1935* by T. S. Eliot, copyright 1936 by Harcourt, Brace & World, Inc.; and to *The New York Times Magazine* for permission to quote "Life I Lived" by Ernest Raymond, in the issue of September 27, 1959, copyright 1959 by *The New York Times.*

Library of Congress Catalog Number 77-70182
Copyright 1961 Howard Thurman
Harper & Row edition 1961
Friends United Press edition published 1971. Fifth printing 1986.
ISBN 0-913408-03-4

To

CHANNING H. TOBIAS

A fruitful tree by a well of water
Whose branches hang over the fence.

FOREWORD

This is volume three of *Deep Is the Hunger*. These meditations were written originally for the weekly *Bulletin* of Marsh Chapel, Boston University, as a part of its ministry. Each one has been used by many people within the University and the larger community beyond its walls. In the course of a year, a host of people from our own country and beyond the seas attend the Sunday morning religious services in Marsh Chapel. Each Sunday morning the congregation consists of persons from the Orient, Africa, the Near East, Europe, South America, Canada, and the United States. This fact has influenced the character of the meditations. For the most part, they are addressed to the deepest needs and aspirations of the human spirit. Their purpose is to make articulate the authentic lines along which the individual's spiritual quest has led him through the years.

A special word is in order concerning the prose poems on I Corinthians 13 and Psalm 139. The intent here is to take some aspect of the meaning of a particular verse and develop it into a creative overtone which conveys its own insight. The brooding mood in which each is cast is an accurate expression of my own personal response to the impact of the verses.

There are not many windows in these meditations; they are as the title indicates, an Inward Journey. It may be that if there were more illustrations, the meaning could be more quickly grasped. The choice here is deliberate. It is my hope that they will make reading and rereading rewarding and sustaining. The purpose remains ever the same: to focus the mind and the heart upon God as the Eternal Source and Goal of Life. To find Him as Companion and Presence is "to do justly, and to love mercy, and to walk humbly" with Him.

To all who have shared their reactions to these meditations either with piercing criticism, simple gratitude, or searching question, I give my thanks. A particular gratitude goes to my wife, Sue Bailey Thurman, whose mind and spirit are ever alert to distinguish between the commonplace and the authentic; to my daughter, Anne Spencer Thurman, who brought to bear upon the pages of the manuscript a journalistic sensitiveness to the written word; to Sydna Altschuler who typed and retyped the manuscript and whose quiet understanding of the "book process" was ever helpful; and to my secretary, Elizabeth Ballard, who week after week has the uninspiring task of reading the original penciled copy of the meditation and preparing it for the Sunday *Bulletin.* My special appreciation goes to the Coleman Jennings Fellowship of Edinbergh, Scotland, whose guests Mrs. Thurman and I were for two months during which time these pages were first put in manuscript order.

H. T.

Marsh Chapel
Boston University

CONTENTS

THE QUEST FOR FULFILLMENT

THE QUEST FOR LOVE

I Corinthians 13

THE QUEST FOR PEACE

THE QUEST FOR GOD

PSALM 139

The Quest for Meaning

Inherent in life is meaning.

1. Meaning Is Inherent in Life

INHERENT in life is meaning. This is a quality, independent of the way in which outside forces may operate upon life. The life in the seed bursts forth in root and stalk and fruit—the whole process takes place within. Many forces may operate upon it from without—cramping the roots, making the shape of the stalk into a caricature of itself—but always with whatever life there is, the built-in purpose is never given up. Concerning this meaning there is no doubt, wherever life appears. This is the integrity of life, it is the commitment of life; this is the singular characteristic of all aliveness; this is the miracle, the shaping of matter from within: the materializing of vitality. The total experience seems to take place in a manner so pervasive that we look in vain for the center, the location of the secret.

Can life's experience of itself at the level of tree and plant, cat and dog, even in the body of man, be also life's experience of itself at the level of the mind? Is there a meaning inherent in the life of the mind itself that is the unfolding of an inner logic not to be accounted for in terms of stimulus from the outside or of response to the outside? May it be that all the dreams, the hopes, the creative flashes like summer lightning, which do not ever quite desert the human mind, are inherent in the mind itself as meaning characteristic of the life in the mind? Wherever life appears it carries with it meaning which is characteristic of all vitality—life means inherent order, built-in goals, purposes, patterns, or designs. These, however simple, determine the form of the life. When the form of life becomes more complex, this fact too is reflected in the pattern, the design, the purpose, the inherent aim.

It may be that in the mind of man, in the rich diversity and depth of human thought, in the searching restlessness for which the word "spirit" seems more appropriate, the life inherent is moving always toward goals and ends that are sensed only when realized. And beyond all these there may be a life of mankind which is more than individuals and groups but in which there is the built-in purpose, aim, and goal. Such purposes, aims, and goals may have increasing creativity as their inherent characteristic. Perhaps this is why we seem always to be presented with goals that can never be realized and ends which can never be fulfilled. Thus the ultimate word which is reserved for God is Creator—the creative act must ever be the personal act.

2. The Innocent Ones

ONE of the characters in Margaret Kennedy's novel *The Feast* suggests that the entire human race is tolerated for its innocent minority. There is a strange and aweful vitality in the suffering of the innocent. It does not fall within any category. The mind moves very easily in the balance of the swinging pendulum. We are accustomed to equating things in terms of the order of equilibrium. Our values are defined most easily as merit and demerit, reward and punishment. There is great sustenance for the spirit in the assurance that reverses can somehow be balanced by the deeds which brought them about. Many men find the depths of contentment in their suffering when they remember that their pain is deserved, their payment is for a just and honest debt. Of course there may be a full measure, pressed down and overflowing, but the hard core of the pain is for acknowledged wrong done; the essence of the hardship is atonement for evil done. All of this falls into a simple pattern of checks and balances, of sowing and reaping, of planting and harvesting.

But where the pain is without apparent merit, where innocence abounds and no case can be made that will give a sound basis for the *experience of the agony,* then the mind spins in a crazy circle. Always there must be an answer, there must be found some clue to the mystery of the suffering of the innocent. It is not enough to say that the fathers have eaten sour grapes and their children's teeth are set on edge. This is not enough. It is not enough to say that the individual

15

sufferer is a victim of circumstances over which he is unable to exercise any controls. There is apt ever to be an element of truth in such assertions. But the heart of the issue remains untouched. The innocent do suffer; this is the experience of man.

Margaret Kennedy's idea is an arresting one. It is that mankind is protected and sustained by undeserved suffering—that swinging out beyond the logic of antecedent and consequence, of sowing and reaping, there is another power, another force, supplementing and restoring the ravages wrought in human life by punishment and reward. The innocent ones are always present when the payment falls due— they are not heroes or saints, they are not those who are the conscious burden-bearers of the sins and transgressions of men. They are the innocent ones—they are always there. Their presence in the world is the stabilizing factor, the precious ingredient that maintains the delicate balance preventing humanity from plunging into the abyss. It is not to be wondered at that in all the religions of mankind there is ever at work the movement to have the word *made* flesh, without being *of* the flesh. It is humanity's way of *affirming* that the innocent ones *hold* while all that evil men do exacts its due.

> Their shoulders hold the sky suspended,
> They stand, and earth's foundations stay

3. When Knowledge Comes

THE SETTING is the Garden of Eden. Adam and Eve are the central figures in an idyllic surrounding. All is peaceful. All is innocent. They are told by God that they are free to do anything except one thing. They are forbidden to eat the fruit of the tree of knowledge which grows in the midst of the garden. For if they eat of the fruit they shall be driven from the garden and from that day forward they shall be responsible for their own lives. They eat of the fruit; they are driven out of the garden; they become responsible for their own lives. With the coming of knowledge, they have lost their innocence.

The transition from innocence to knowledge is always perilous

16

and balmy. It is to live in the calm of the eye of the hurricane. It is to live in a static environment which makes upon the individual no demands other than to *be*. All else is cared for; is guaranteed.

But when knowledge comes, the whole world is turned upside down. The meaning of things begins to emerge. And more importantly, the relations between things are seen for the first time. Questions are asked and answers are sought. A strange restlessness comes over the spirit and the enormity of error moves over the horizon like a vast shadow. Struggle emerges as the way of life. An appetite is awakened that can never be satisfied. A person becomes conscious of himself; the urge to know, to understand, to find answers, turns inward. Every estimate of others becomes a question of self-estimate, every judgment upon life becomes a self-judgment. The question of the meaning of one's self becomes one with the meaning of life.

This process of moving from innocence to knowledge is never finished. Always there is the realm of innocence, always there is the realm of knowledge. Always there is some area of innocence untouched by knowledge. The more profound the growth of knowledge, the more aware the individual becomes of the dimensions of innocence. Pride in knowledge is always tempered by the dominion of innocence. Often we do not become aware of innocence until we experience knowledge.

The setting is the Garden of Eden. Adam and Eve are the central figures in an idyllic surrounding. All is peaceful. All is innocent. They are told by God that they are free to do anything except one thing. They are forbidden to eat the fruit of the tree of knowledge which grows in the midst of the garden. For if they eat of the fruit they shall be driven from the garden and from that day forward they shall be responsible for their own lives. They eat of the fruit; they are driven out of the garden; they become responsible for their own lives.

FIERCE INDEED is the grip by which we hold on to our lives as our private possession. The struggle to achieve some sense of individuality in the midst of other people and other things is grim. We are always surrounded by persons, forces, and objects which lay siege to us and seek to make of us means to their ends or at least to their fulfillment. The demand is ever present to distinguish between the self and the not-self.

There are moments of enthusiasm when with mounting excitement we absorb ourselves in something beyond ourselves. But after this happens we fight at length to get back home, to come again into the familiar place, to be secure in our own boundaries. Again and again the process repeats itself, wearing down the walls that shut us in.

Of course, a man may, by early resolution, frustration, or bitter experience, withdraw more and more from all involvements. By this process he seeks to immunize himself against hurts and from what seems to be certain disaster. Behold such a man! His spirit shrinks, his mind becomes ingrown, his imagination turns inward. The wall surrounding him becomes so thick that deep within he is threatened with isolation. This is the threat of death. Sometimes his spirit breaks out in reverse by giving voices to inward impulses, thus establishing by the sheer will to survival a therapy for the corrosion of his spirit.

For all of this religion has a searching word. "Deep within are the issues of life." "The rule of God is within." "If thou hadst known the things which belong unto thy peace." There is a surrender of the life that redeems, purifies, and makes whole. Every surrender to a particular person, event, circumstance, or activity is but a token surrender, the temporary settling of the life in security. These are not to be ignored but they are all passing and transitory. They end in tightening the wall of isolation around the spirit. They are too narrow, too limited, and finally unworthy.

The surrender must be to something big enough to absolve one

18

only by something that gathers up into itself all meaning and all value. It is the claim of religion that this is found only in God. The pathways vary but the goal is One.

5. Radical Amazement

ABRAHAM HESCHEL, in his book *Man Is Not Alone,* uses a very telling phrase, "radical amazement." He is talking about the experience of encountering that which is direct, overwhelming, and ineffable. It is what remains when all externals are stripped away and the individual has a naked exposure at his deepest level to something that envelops him and stands him at attention.

We have externalized our lives to such an extent that, more and more, the only real things seem to be what we can touch, see, hear, taste, and smell. As long as we are dealing with objects at the level of the senses we think that we are on ground that is safe and therefore certain. This tendency expresses itself in many ways. We measure our friendship by a wide variety of tokens of testing: by the things we are given, by the repetition of words of affection, by the obvious sacrifices made in our behalf. We often place value upon ourselves in terms of the extent and quality of our wardrobe or by the size of our bank account or by the number of prestige-bearing people who know us and recognize us or by the power we are able to exert over things. Each of us makes his own list.

What is forgotten is the fact that life moves at a deeper level than the objective and the data of our senses. We are most alive when we are brought face to face with the response of the deepest thing in us to the deepest thing in life. Consider the hackneyed illustration of the beautiful sunset! We see the sunset, we recognize color, shape, the general quality of the atmosphere—to these we respond. Then when in the midst of all of this something else emerges—the sunset opens a door in us and to us, to another dimension, timeless in quality, that can be described only as ineffable, awe-inspiring—then we are literally catapulted out of the narrow walls that shut us in. We experience radical amazement. Spirit is met by Spirit and we are whole again!

6. No Experience Contains All

THERE is something strange and awesome about the quality of mind that keeps it from coming to rest within any single idea, or any single experience. No deed which we have experienced, however good and wonderful it may be, can quite contain all that we meant by the thing we have done. No word that we have ever uttered can express fully and adequately what we were trying to say. No goal that we have ever set before us and achieved is ever capable of containing all that we were seeking. There always remains a residue that does not ever get itself contained by any vessel we may use whether it be a thought, an idea, a deed, a goal, a dream, or even a life. The *something more* cries out for expression and the expression does not ever quite come off.

In the entire gamut of our relationship with one another this experience of man is written large. There is a time when we dream of the perfect relationship—the perfect union, the perfect friendship, the perfect love. Standing in the first full flush of the newness of love we are often so overcome by the vast release of life and joy that we are convinced that what others have felt only dimly, is ours in all its glory and completeness. This is good! This is wonderful! There is more to our feelings than we are expressing, there is more in our vision of love than we are experiencing—however slowly something else begins to emerge. We cannot escape the sure persistent sense of inadequacy—however hard we try. Even when our offering of the self is completely accepted and we are to another person far more than he ever dreamed that anyone would or could ever be to him, the fact remains that what we are giving is only partial, what we are sharing is less, much less, than is our desiring.

Therefore, to put into the deed less than the best; to give to the relationship only a shadow of the self; to put at the disposal of the dream only that which is fragmentary and ineffective is to spend one's days stumbling through the darkness. If a man's best is never quite within his grasp, the less than best is woefully inadequate. There is ever the hope that what the mind searches for today but does not quite succeed in finding, will be its strength and stay tomorrow and tomorrow and tomorrow.

7. Accept Our Fact

OFTEN it is most difficult to accept our fact. Such acceptance means to say "yes" to that which is our own bill of particulars. It does not begin with embracing in some grand manner the great world of which we are a part—even though it may include that, ultimately. It does not mean the recognition of our membership in the human race —although it may include that, ultimately. It means being very specific about ourselves. This is our face, not another's; it will always be our face exhibiting a countenance that reveals all the laughter and all the tears of our years of living. Whatever a face means in the history of the human race, all the face-meaning which is uniquely ours is ours as utterly as if there were no face on earth except our own. No substitute can be found for it—go where we will, knock at every door, our face remains our face. This is an item of our bill of particulars.

Our situation is uniquely our own. True, we may be victims of circumstances. The operation of forces that did not take our needs into account may have marred our lives and twisted our personalities out of harmony with our intent and our dream. All of this may be an accurate description of our experience of life. If there had been some hand to raise itself in our behalf at the moment of crisis, how different would our whole world be. But there was no hand. There was only we and the cutting edge of the moment with nothing be-tween. All through the years the scar tissue has marked the place. We cannot forget. Our situation is uniquely our own.

Often more difficult than to *accept* our fact is to learn how to *deal* with our fact. It is here that the resources of our lives are brought to bear. It may be that we reject all resources as of no avail and we abandon our self to our fact, taking refuge in bitterness and despair. Our heart grows cold and life becomes a great and unyielding weariness.

Or we may draw upon all skills and understandings outside of and beyond ourselves, seeking always to alter our fact in ways that are both creative and redemptive. This may happen after we have exhausted our own inner vitalities to that end. If all of these fail then we must learn how to live with our fact, to domesticate it and make of it a friend. In all ages men have found in religion access to God who companions them in such struggles, giving not only comfort and reassurance, but also strength and courage. To discover this is to say "yes" to Life and to our life.

8. Belief and Faith

THERE seems to be a valid distinction between belief and faith. Often we think of belief as having to do exclusively with a body of ideas, notions, concepts, or the like. The term is identical with dogma and creed. But it is not that aspect of belief that is always decisive in living. There is a simpler definition of belief that carries with it a meaning well within the experience of all who live: A man's belief is what he does, what he practices. It is no mere matter of the mind and its assent; it is not the thing to which a man subscribes as a part of the membership requirements of an institution to which he belongs. Rather, it is the nature and the kind of response which he makes to the current demands of his life; it is the design that such responses make when viewed as a whole; it is the inner consistency of his basic behavior.

There is nothing accidental or incidental about beliefs. They determine and yet are determined by the set of a man's spirit. This is the strange paradox. Out of the deep places of a man's heart flow the issues by which he lives. The issues by which he lives are deeply "qualitied" by the things that he does with consistency.

On the other hand, faith has an element that is given. It seems to have no beginning and no ending. It does not spring from sources that are under the control of the individual nor responsible to his life. Faith gathers in its sweep the life of man, as indeed all that lives, and informs it with overtones of hope and anticipations of the future. It holds within its grasp the past and the future as a single moment in time. It does not seek to secure itself by the sanction of mind or by a denial of the necessity of thought. It does not fortify itself with sanctions of proof or rest its case on the generosity of demonstration. Faith envelops life and charges it with energy that sustains and holds. It is the breath of God that becomes in all living things the breath of Life.

9. The Experience of Ingathering

THE EXPERIENCE of ingathering, of collection, of recollection, is to be coveted beyond all reckoning. It is a time of searching and of appraisal. We enter that Open Door as we center our spirits in Meditation and Prayer:

We hold in a special place of tenderness those who have suffered deeply from great violences, families that are bereft because of death caused by murder and the angry spirit; families that are distraught because of illnesses which do not respond to any of the incisive and technical ministry of the hand skilled in healing and the mind disciplined in the art of therapy.

We cradle in our love those who inhabit the shadows where things are never clear, where the mind seems enveloped in heavy fog and at the core of the spirit is the submerged torture that makes ever for restlessness and unrelieved madness; the children who are this day without love and compassion, who are driven to deal with life as if they were mature and who move hour by hour in a daze of bewilderment, destitution, anguish, and fear; the lonely who somehow cannot experience the penetration of the wall by which they are enclosed and are thus rendered stranded, forlorn; and those who are tired, the very ground of whose being seems exhausted by a great weariness, with all the springs of renewal dried up at the source—all of these crowd in upon us in the stillness of this waiting moment.

God, close present Father, we do not know how to ask of Thee, we do not know what to say: Thou wilt give speech to our needs. We offer both the cloud of witnesses to human need and our concern, to Thee for Sanctuary, Healing, and Redemption. We wait for the movement of Thy Spirit in our hearts and in our minds that we may be led into paths of service as Thy living agents. Grant, our Father, that we may not betray Thy urgency either through self-love, self-pity or fear—this our souls cannot abide. Deliver us from so great a temptation. Amen.

10. A Good Death

"I WANT to die easy when I die." This is a line from an old song which belonged to another period and another age. There is no gruesome note here, not a single morbid or depressing overtone. We are not face to face with something that is grim and foreboding. But we are faced with a grand conception of death that gathers in its sweep all the little fears and anxieties that condition the personal view and the private contemplation of the end of life. It is a Trumpet Call to human dignity.

The madder the world seems, the more the rumors of lethal devices reach our ears, the more we are desirous of finding and clinging to a few simple values: things that can be felt and held and owned; a bit of economic security, transitory though it be, that will give a few rare moments free of the immediate necessity of working for that day's bread; the experience of love, however fleeting, and perchance a family as a primary defense against not being wanted and not belonging. So strenuous is our pursuit for these things that it is difficult even to grasp the great concept which the line presents to the human spirit—"I want to die easy when I die."

Life and death are felt as a single respiration—the ebb and flow of a single tide. Death is not the invasion of an alien principle, it is not an attack upon life by an enemy. Death is not the Grim

Reaper, the black-cowled skeleton with blazing eyes, galloping on a white horse. No! Life and death are identical twins. Therefore it is man's privilege and wisdom to make a good death, even as it is to make a good life.

A good death is made up of the same elements as a good life. A good life is what a man does with the details of living if he sees his life as an instrument, a deliberate instrument in the hands of Life, that transcends all boundaries and all horizons. It is this *beyond dimension* that saves the individual life from being swallowed by the tyranny of present needs, present hungers, and present threats. This is to put distance *within* the experience and to live the quality of the beyond even in the intensity of the present moment. And a good death—what is it? It has the same quality and character as a good life. True, the body may be stripped of all defenses by the ravages of disease; there may remain no surface expression of dignity and self-respect as the organism yields slowly to the pressure of change monitored by death. These are all secondary. The real issue is at another depth entirely. It is at the place where Life has been long since accepted and yielded to, where the private will has become infused with the Great Will, where the child of God realizes his Sonship. This is the knowledge that the son has of the Father and the Father of the son—this is to know God and to abide in Him forever.

11. The Fall of the Year

FOR MANY of us the fall of the year is a time of sadness and the long memory. All around us there are the evidences of fading, of withdrawal, of things coming to an end. What was alive and growing only a few short days or weeks ago seems now to have fulfilled itself and fallen back into the shadows. Vegetation withers but there is no agony of departure; there seems to be only death and stillness in the fall.

Those who have been ill all summer seem to get a deepening sense of foreboding in the fall. It is the time of the changing of the guard. It is the season of the retreat of energy. It is a time of letting go. It is the period of the first exhaustion. It is the period of the storms, as if the wind itself becomes the Avenging Angel too impatient to wait for the coming of death and the quiet fading of bud and flower and leaf. The rain is not gentle in the fall, it is feverish, truculent, and vicious. All the fury of wind and rain are undertoned by a vast lull in tempo and the running down of all things. There is a chill in the air in the fall. It is not cold; it is chilly, as if the temperature cannot quite make up its mind. The chill is ominous, the forerunner of the vital coldness of winter.

But the fall of the year is more than all this; much, much more. It marks an important change in the cycle of the year. This change means that summer is passed. One season ends by blending into another. Here is a change of pace accenting a rhythm in the passing of time. How important this is! The particular mood inspires recollection and reflection. There is something very steadying and secure in the awareness that there is an underlying dependability in life—that change is a part of the experience of living. It is a reminder of the meaning of pause and plateau.

But fall provides something more. There is a harvest, a time of ingathering, of storing up in nature; there is a harvest, a time of ingathering, of storing up in the heart. There is the time when there must be a separation of that which has said its say and passes—that which ripens and finds its meaning in sustaining life in other forms. Nothing is lost, nothing disappears; all things belong, each in its way, to a harmony and an order which envelops all, which infuses all.

Fall accentuates the goodness of life and finds its truest meaning in the strength of winter and the breath of spring. Thank God for the fall.

12. Chanukah and Christmas

THERE must always remain in every people's life some space for the celebration of those events of the past that bear their fruit in the present—those events in which the race seems to catch its breath and to give the long look forward and backward. Such events are surrounded by a quality all their own, and yet they seem to gather into themselves the essence of all striving and the meaning of all hope.

Chanukah is such an event. Here was a moment in the life of Israel in which a people was faced with an ultimate choice. On the one hand, to renounce the very heart of a faith in One God with whom they were covenanted and to give a false value to a profound communal commitment. On the other hand, to say "yes" to a truth by which the steps of the past had been guided when there was no light, and no guide save one. One man in his vision became, first, a whole nation and then the whole race of mankind, as he affirmed in his deed: the Lord God is one and alone is worthy to be worshiped and to be praised. From him has come a way that, for generations of men, has become The Way.

Christmas is such an event. Here was a moment in the life of Israel in which a baby was born in surroundings as commonplace as the leaves and branches of the olive tree. In him was seen, by many, that for which their hearts had hungered and of which their dreams had foretold. He grew into manhood exhibiting in word and deed a fresh new quality of the age-old response of the spirit of man to the call of God. God was everything to him. His was the vision of a great creative ideal that all men are children of God, that the normal relation of one man to another is love (anything else is against life), and that there is a personal Power, God, equally available to rich and poor, to Jew and Gentile, to men and women, to the wise and the foolish, to the just and the unjust. For millions his birth marks the turning point in human history. Christmas is an event, above all events, for it marks the moment when a new meaning is given to ancient words: The eyes of the blind are opened, the captive are set free, and the acceptable year of the Lord is become literal truth!

Chanukah and Christmas spring from the same womb and are mothered by the same brooding spirit: one marks freedom from tyranny and the preservation of the Eternal Light for all the generations of men; the other announces that there is a Presence in the common life, a Light that lighteth every man that cometh into the world.

13. What Is Christmas?

CHRISTMAS is a mood, a quality, a symbol. It is never merely a fact. As a fact it is a date on the calendar; to the believer it is the anniversary of the Event in human history. An individual may relate himself meaningfully to the fact or to the Event, but that would not make Christmas.

The mood of Christmas—what is it? It is a quickening of the presence of other human beings into whose lives a precious part of one's own has been released. It is a memory of other days when in one's path an angel appeared spreading a halo over an ordinary moment or a commonplace event. It is an iridescence of sheer delight that once bathed one's whole being with something more wonderful than words can ever tell. Of such is the mood of Christmas.

The quality of Christmas—what is it? It is the fullness with which fruit ripens, blossoms unfold into flowers, and live coals glow in the darkness. It is the richness of vibrant colors—the calm purple of grapes, the exciting redness of tomatoes, the shimmering light of the noiseless stirring of a lake at sunset. It is the sense of plateau behind a large rock where one may take temporary respite from winds that chill. Of such is the quality of Christmas.

The symbol of Christmas—what is it? It is the rainbow arched over the roof of the sky when the clouds are heavy with foreboding. It is the cry of life in the newborn babe when, forced from its mother's nest, it claims its right to live. It is the brooding Presence of the Eternal Spirit making crooked paths straight, rough places smooth, tired hearts refreshed, dead hopes stirred with the newness of life. It is the promise of tomorrow at the close of every day, the movement of life in defiance of death, and the assurance that love is sturdier than hate, that right is more confident than wrong, that good is more permanent than evil.

I WILL light the candle of fellowship this Christmas. I know that the experiences of unity in human relations are more compelling than the concepts, the fears, the prejudices, which divide. Despite the tendency to feel my race superior, my nation the greatest nation, my faith the true faith, I must beat down the boundaries of my exclusiveness until my sense of separateness is completely enveloped in a sense of fellowship. There must be free and easy access by all, to all the rich resources accumulated by groups and individuals in years of living and experiencing. I will light the candle of fellowship this Christmas a candle that must burn all the year long.

I will light the candle of hope this Christmas. There is strange irony in the fact that there seemed to have existed a more secure basis for hope in the world during the grimmest days of the war than in the vast uncertainties of the postwar and cold war world. Now millions of people are thrown back upon themselves for food which they do not possess, for resources that have long since been exhausted, for vitality which has already run its course. The miracle of fulfillment dreamed of by the uprooted and persecuted masses of men, women and children takes now the form of a hideous nightmare, as peace is so long deferred. But hope is the mood of Christmas; the raw materials are a newborn babe, a family, and work. Even in the grimness of the postwar world, babies are being born—an endless procession that is life's answer to death. Life keeps coming on, keeps seeking to fulfill itself, keeps affirming the possibility of hope.

Hope is the growing edge! I shall look well to that growing edge this Christmas. All around worlds are dying out, new worlds are being born; all around life is dying but life is being born. The fruit ripens on the trees, while the roots are silently at work in the darkness of the earth against a time when there shall be new leaves, fresh blossoms, green fruit. Such is the growing edge! It is the one more thing to try when all else has failed, the upward reach of life. It is the incentive to carry on. Therefore, I will light the candle of hope this Christmas, that must burn all the year long.

To Jesus, God breathed through all that is. The sparrow overcome by sudden death in its evening flight; the lily blossoming on the rocky hillside; the grass of the field and the garden path; the clouds light and burdenless or weighted down with unshed waters; the madman in chains or wandering among the barren rocks in the wastelands; the little baby in his mother's arms; the strutting arrogance of the Roman Legion; the brazen queries of the craven tax collector; the children at play or the old men quibbling in the market place; the august Sanhedrin fighting for its life amidst the impudences of Empire; the futile whisper of those who had forgotten Jerusalem; the fear-voiced utterance of the prophets who remembered—to Jesus, God breathed through all that is. To Jesus, God was Creator of life and the living substance; the Living Stream upon which all things moved; the Mind containing time, space, and all their multitudinous offsprings. And beyond all these God was Friend and Father.

The time most precious for him was at close of day. This was the time for the long breath, when all the fragments left by the commonplace, when all the little hurts and the big aches could be absorbed, and the mind could be freed of the immediate demand, when voices that had been quieted by the long day's work could once more be heard, when there could be the deep sharing of the innermost secrets and the laying bare of the heart and mind. Yes, the time most precious for him was at close of day.

But there were other times he treasured, "A great while before day," says the Book. The night had been long and wearisome because the day had been full of nibbling annoyances; the high resolve of some winged moment had frenzied, panicked, no longer sure, no longer free, and then had vanished as if it had never been. There was need, the utter urgency, for some fresh assurance, the healing touch of a healing wing. "A great while before day" he found his way to the quiet place in the hills. And prayed.

SEARCHING indeed must have been the thoughts moving through the mind of the Master as he jogged along on the back of the donkey on that fateful day which marks in the Christian calendar the Triumphant Entry. The experience must have been as strange and out of character for him as it was for the faithful animal on whose back he rode.

For more than two years, Jesus had been engaged in a public ministry. Once when there were those who wanted to make him a king, he had refused. "My kingdom is not of this world." He had walked the countryside with his band of disciples, preaching, teaching, healing, and spreading a quality of radiance that could come only from one whose overwhelming enthusiasm was for God and His Kingdom. He had kept many lonely trysts in the late watches of the night, trueing his spirit and his whole life by the will of his Father. So close had he worked with God that the line of demarcation between his will and God's Will would fade and reappear, fade and reappear. Step by resolute step, he had come to the great city. Deep within his spirit there may have been a sense of foreboding, or the heightened quality of exhilaration that comes from knowing that there is no road back.

He had learned much. So sensitive had grown his spirit and the living quality of his being that he seemed more and more to stand inside of life, looking out upon it as a man who gazes from a window in a room out into the yard and beyond to the distant hills. He could feel the sparrowness of the sparrow, the leprosy of the leper, the blindness of the blind, the crippleness of the cripple, and the frenzy of the mad. He had become joy, sorrow, hope, anguish, to the joyful, the sorrowful, the hopeful, the anguished. Could he feel his way into the mind and the mood of those who cast the palms and the flowers in his path? Was he in the cry of those who exclaimed their wild and unrestrained Hosannas? Did he mingle with the emotions that lay beneath the exultations ready to explode in the outburst of the mob screaming, "Crucify him! Crucify him!" I wonder what was at work ing the sawdust between his toes, in his father's shop. He may have been remembering the high holy days in the synagogue, with his whole body quickened by the echo of the ram's horn as it sounded. Or perhaps he was thinking of his mother, how deeply he loved her and how he wished that there had not been laid upon him the Great Necessity which sent him out on the open road to proclaim the Truth, leaving her side forever. It may be that he lived all over again that high moment on the Sabbath when he was handed the scroll and he unrolled it to the great passage from the prophet Isaiah, "The spirit of the Lord is upon me, for he has anointed me to preach the gospel to the poor, to open the eyes of the blind, to unstop the ears of the deaf, to announce the acceptable year of the Lord." I wonder what was moving through the mind of the Master as he jogged along the back of the faithful donkey.

The Quest for Understanding

There is a given element in life.

The Quest for Understanding

There is a given element in life.

17. A New Heaven and a New Earth

WE ARE in varied ways concerned about welfare and well-being—our own and that of others. Rare indeed is the man who looks at his own life, who examines his personal position, and is assured that he is in no need of improvement. The place where a man stands is never quite the place that marks the limit of his powers and the resting point for all his dreams. This is the way of life.

It is easier to be more concerned about the welfare and well-being of the world than about our own. Few can escape the urge to join in the general chorus of the age that we have fallen upon evil days. There seems to be a strange, weary comfort in taking one's place against the wailing wall. There is a searching danger ever present in all anxiety, whether personal or social. It can so easily become a substitute for thoughtful planning and action. One is constantly placed in jeopardy by this possibility. Have you ever said with real feeling, "I must do something about drinking so much coffee" or "I am alarmed over the fact that I can't seem to get down to business with my own personal life"? Of the great number of people who feel outraged over what seems to be a terrible miscarriage of justice, how many do something concrete about it? All the energy is exhausted in such remarks: "How awful"—"What a tragedy"—"Something ought to be done"—"What a shame."

Again, our emotional reaction to situations causes us to adopt measures that bring quick and temporary relief from the immediate pressures on us but do not have much effect on the situations themselves. The real purpose is to relieve only ourselves. Somehow we must find that which is big enough to absolve us from artificial and ineffective methods for increasing welfare and well-being. This means the large view, the great faith, which will release the vast courage

34

capable of sustaining us in the long pull toward a valid increase in welfare and well-being. It is for this reason that a religious faith about life and its meaning becomes a necessity for all who would work for a new heaven and a new earth, the achievement of which is literal fact.

18. The Experience of Love

THERE is a steady anxiety that surrounds man's experience of love. Sometimes the radiance of love is so soft and gentle that the individual sees himself with all harsh lines wiped away and all limitations blended with his strengths in so happy a combination that strength seems to be everywhere and weakness is nowhere to be found. This is a part of the magic, the spell of love. Sometimes the radiance of love kindles old fires that have long since grown cold from the neglect of despair, or new fires are kindled by a hope born full-blown without beginning and without ending. Sometimes the radiance of love blesses a life with a vision of its possibilities never before dreamed of or sought, stimulating new endeavor and summoning all latent powers to energize the life at its inmost core.

But there are other ways by which love works its perfect work. It may stab the spirit by calling forth a bitter, scathing self-judgment. The heights to which it calls may seem so high that all incentive is lost and the individual is stricken with an utter hopelessness and despair. It may throw in relief old and forgotten weaknesses to which one has made the adjustment of acceptance—but which now stir in their place to offer themselves as testimony of one's unworthiness and to challenge the love with their embarrassing authenticity. It is at such times that one expects love to be dimmed under the mistaken notion that love is at long last based upon merit and worth.

Behold the miracle! Love has no awareness of merit or demerit; it has no scale by which its portion may be weighed or measured. It does not seek to balance giving and receiving. Love loves; this is its nature. But this does not mean that love is blind, naïve, or pretentious. It does mean that love holds its object securely in its grasp, calling all that it sees by its true name but surrounding all with a wisdom born

both of its passion and its understanding. Here is no traffic in sentimentality, no catering to weakness or to strength. Instead, there is
robust vitality that quickens the roots of personality, creating an unfolding of the self that redefines, reshapes, and makes all things new.
Such an experience is so fundamental in quality that an individual
knows that what is happening to him can outlast all things without
itself being dissipated or lost.

Whence comes this power which seems to be the point of referral
for all experience and the essence of all meaning? No created thing,
no single unit of life, can be the source of such fullness and completeness. For in the experience itself a man is caught and held by
something so much more than he can ever think or be that there is
but one word by which its meaning can be encompassed—God.
Hence the Psalmist says that as long as the love of God shines on us
undimmed, not only may no darkness obscure but also we may find
our way to a point in other hearts beyond all weakness and all strength,
beyond all that is good and beyond all that is evil. There is no thing
outside ourselves, no circumstance, no condition, no vicissitude, that
can ultimately separate us from the love of God and from the love of
one another. And we pour out our gratitude to God that this is so!

19. Given Element in Life

THERE is a given element in life. The moment when life becomes
life is no man's secret. The moment when life becomes life can
never be known. All around us we see evidences of life-movement,
forms, structures, in combination, in context. Within ourselves we
feel life, it *is* already. Wrapped within it, there seems to be a vast
energy without beginning and without end. There is a given element
in life.

What is it? All that is ours to know is that life itself is alive. To
experience this is to live; it is to feel pulsing through the body energy,
vitality, power. It is to feel the lift of the mind to heights of understanding and clarity. It is to walk in the strength of a faith restored
and a dream that has come to life. It is to continue to give when there
is no more to give. It is to hold fast, sometimes against all evidence

and all odds. It is to lose everything and yet remain secure against all disaster.

I have wondered about this strange quality of renewal that is one with life itself. May not the clue be nurtured in the fact that life feeds on itself? The grain of corn dies in the earth that the germ hidden away in its core may live, multiply, and bear fruit. All the bloody carnage surrounding the sustaining of life is grounded in the shrieks and cries of the dying as life consumes itself. Life lives on life; this is the way of life. Here may be found the key to the meaning of all sacrifice and the answer to the urge present in every human heart to *give* itself away.

It is only when the mind is farthest removed from its experience of life that death becomes a separate thing. "He that believeth . . . shall never die" is no empty phrase of Christian piety. It is rather a recognition of eternal process inherent in the experience of life itself. Despite the universal character of the fact, the experience itself is always private, always personal. The *shadow* of death of which the Psalmist speaks is the thing that strikes the terror, the resounding echo of which leaves no ear unassailed. But death itself has no such power because the experience of life contains the fact of death. There is a given element in life—it is the givenness of God. To know this thoroughly is to rob death of its terror and life of its fear.

20. A Strange Freedom

It is a strange freedom to be adrift in the world of men without a sense of anchor anywhere. Always there is the need of mooring, the need for the firm grip on something that is rooted and will not give. The urge to be accountable to someone, to know that beyond the individual himself there is an answer that must be given, cannot be denied. The deed a man performs must be weighed in a balance held by another's hand. The very spirit of a man tends to panic from the desolation of going nameless up and down the streets of other minds where no salutation greets and no friendly recognition makes secure. It is a strange freedom to be adrift in the world of men.

Always a way must be found for bringing into one's solitary place the settled look from another's face, for getting the quiet sanction of another's grace to undergird the meaning of the self. To be ignored, to be passed over as of no account and of no meaning, is to be made into a faceless thing, not a man. It is better to be the complete victim of an anger unrestrained and a wrath which knows no bounds, to be torn asunder without mercy or battered to a pulp by angry violence, then to be passed over as if one were not. Here at least one is dealt with, encountered, vanquished, or overwhelmed—but not ignored. It is a strange freedom to go nameless up and down the streets of other minds where no salutation greets and no sign is given to mark the place one calls one's own.

The name marks the claim a man stakes against the world; it is the private banner under which he moves which is his right whatever else betides. The name is a man's water mark above which the tides can never rise. It is the thing he holds that keeps him in the way when every light has failed and every marker has been destroyed. It is the rallying point around which a man gathers all that he means by himself. It is his announcement to life that he is present and accounted for in all his parts. To be made anonymous and to give to it the acquiescence of the heart is to live without life, and for such a one, even death is no dying.

To be known, to be called by one's name, is to find one's place and hold it against all the hordes of hell. This is to *know* one's value, for one's self alone. It is to honor an act as one's very own, it is to live a life that is one's very own, it is to bow before an altar that is one's very own, it is to worship a God who is one's very own.

It is a strange freedom to be adrift in the world of men, to act with no accounting, to go nameless up and down the streets of other minds where no salutation greets and no sign is given to mark the place one calls one's own.

21. Life Must Be Experienced

IN MANY ways modern man lives his life as a bystander. Again and again we are several steps removed from the primary experiences of living. When a person becomes critically ill, under most circumstances he is taken from the bosom of his family to a hospital. Here he is given the kind of care and treatment that would be impossible in the home. And this is good. But it means that all of the experience of tenderness that comes from having to care for the sick is denied us. We have little of the winnowing of character that exposes life to the elemental nobility of human nature at bay. The care of the sick often purges the life of self-centeredness and hardness of heart.

When there is death in the family, the body is removed to the funeral establishment. It is no longer the shared responsibility of the members of the family to prepare the body for burial. Many persons live their entire lives without ever seeing a human being die. There is available to us no primary contact with the experience of death as a part of the common life. The great and tragic exception occurs during vast violences like war or the kind of disaster mentioned in bills of lading as Acts of God. Life and death are seen more and more as two separate entities; we cling to one and fear the other.

All of this adds up to a profound distrust of life itself. Life is seen then as being something to conquer, to struggle with and against. Life is the enemy. It is not to be embraced, to be lived. Hence we creep through our days, reacting to our world as if our faith were in magic, rather than in life. Man must experience life; he must feel it run through his whole being that life belongs to him and he to life. The experience *of* life not *in* life will teach a man not to fear life but to love life. He discovers that the test of life in him is to be found in the amount of pain, of frustration, he can absorb without spoiling his joy in living. To keep alive an original sense of aliveness is to know that life is its own restraint and a man is able to stand anything that life can do to him. This is what religion means by faith in God. "O men, how little you trust God."

22. The Self-Encounter

WHEN have you last had a good session with yourself? Or have you ever had it out with *you?*

Most often you are brought face to face with yourself only when such an encounter is forced upon you. Usually it is in connection with a crisis situation. There is a death in the immediate circle of close family or friends with the result that definite changes must be made in your way of living and thinking. You must accustom yourself to living without the active relationship of the departed one. Or it may be that there is the quickening discovery that your parents are old and can no longer relate to you at the point of your needs but you must relate to them at the point of their need.

There may be other causes of self-confrontation. A chance remark from a friend may bring you quickly to face the fact that you are a pretender in your relations with others, that you have never faced up to your own lack of integrity in word and in act. In a time of temper you may say things of which you are deeply ashamed, not so much because you said them—that is bad enough—but because you were capable of thinking them. You may discover that in trying to make a decision involving a course of action, you are utterly incompetent to do so because you have never claimed your mind as your own. All through the years you have drifted from one position to another, letting your meaning be determined by your response to others or their demands—not determined by how you felt, really, nor what you personally thought. Now you look for some clue outside yourself and there is none to be found. *You* must decide and abide.

Whatever may be the occasion there comes a deep necessity which leads you finally into the closet with yourself. It is here that you raise the real questions about yourself. The leading one is, What is it, after all, that I amount to, ultimately? Such a question cuts through all that is superficial and trivial in life to the very nerve center of yourself. And this is a religious question because it deals with the total meaning of life at its heart. At such a moment, and at such a time, you must discover for yourself what is the *true* basis of your self-respect. This is found only in relation to God whose Presence makes itself known in the most lucid moments of self-awareness. For all of us are His children and the most crucial clue to a knowledge of Him is to be found in the most honest and most total knowledge of the self.

23. The Necessities of Our Peace

THERE is a widespread feeling of despair and feeling of futility not only about the present times but also about the future. There are many reasons for this attitude; indeed, the reasons are not far to seek. The cumulative anxiety resulting from two world wars with the vast eruption of hate and misery has left its mark in the soul of the nations of the earth. It is terrible enough when wars are fought by hired mercenaries, but when they become the immediate and personal involvement of young men and women, old men and women, boys and girls, then there is left no one who does not bear the deep bruises and shock of its consequence. The standing peacetime army is more and more taken for granted as the common experience of the modern nation.

There is also the subtle fear spreading like a "pea-soup" fog over the entire landscape of our personalities because of the naked power made available by the unlocking of the prison house of the atom. Suddenly there is an awareness that no one anywhere is safe, that there is no protection for man against what man can do to man and all that he holds dear.

For us in America there is the searching guilt because, alone of the nations of the earth, we have introduced atomic warfare into the organized life of man. It is true that we say again and again that the irony of a fateful extenuating circumstance forced the choice upon us. But the fact remains that the choice was ours. How can so great a stain be purged, how can there be quiet in the heart that remembers Hiroshima?

At such times as these it is good to remember that we are under the necessity to use all of the devices of our democratic process to make our domestic and foreign policies enlightened and morally responsive to a good social conscience. We must remember that at the level of the daily round we must put our own courage, gentleness, and kindly devotion at the disposal of simple community in our homes, in our work, and in our play. The good deed continues to be good, the kind word continues to be kind, the cup of cold water

41

given to the thirsty continues to be refreshing and reassuring—the need for love is as urgent and desperate as it ever was. Faith in life, faith in one's self, faith in one another, faith in God: these are the necessities for our peace.

24. Keep Open the Door of Thy Heart

Keep open the door of thy heart.
It matters not how many doors are closed against thee.

IT IS a wondrous discovery when there is disclosed to the mind the fact that there may be no direct and responsible relation between two human beings that can determine their attitude toward each other. We are accustomed to thinking that one man's attitude toward another is a response to an attitude. The formula is very neat: love begets love, hate begets hate, indifference begets indifference. Often this is true. Again and again we try to mete out to others what we experience at their hands. There is much to be said for the contagion of attitudes. There are moments in every man's life when he tries to give as good or as bad as he gets. But this presupposes that the relation between human beings is somehow mechanical, as if each person is utterly and completely separated. This is far from the truth, even though it may seem to square with *some* of the facts of our experienced behavior.

There is a profound ground of unity that is more pertinent and authentic than all the unilateral dimensions of our lives. This a man discovers when he is able to keep open the door of his heart. This is one's ultimate responsibility, and it is not dependent upon whether the heart of another is kept open for him. Here is a mystery: If sweeping through the door of my heart there moves continually a genuine love for you, it by-passes all your hate and all your indifference and gets through to you at your center. You are powerless to do anything about it. You may keep alive in devious ways the fires of your bitter heart, but they cannot get through to me. Underneath the surface of all the tension, something else is at work. It is utterly impossible for you to keep another from loving you. True, you may scorn his love, you may reject it in all ways within your power, you may try to close every opening in your own heart—it will not matter. This is no easy sentimentality but it is the very essence of the vitality of all being. The word that love is stronger than hate and goes beyond death is the great disclosure to one who has found that when he keeps open the door of his heart, it matters not how many doors are closed against him.

25. The Good Deed

WHAT happens when you do a good deed that meets some urgent need in the life of another person? Do you share with the person anything beyond the deed that is done, beyond the gift that is given?

Does the other person share with you anything beyond the deed that is accepted, beyond the gift that is received? Suppose the deed done and the gift given were the outward expression of an inward urge? Suppose the necessity to give were an inner necessity, generated by the discovery within yourself that your life is marked off from another life by the thinnest lines?

It is a world-shattering disclosure that the stream of life is a single stream, though it takes various forms as it spills over into time and space. This disclosure is made to anyone whose discipline sends him on high adventure within his own spirit, his own inner life. By prayer, by the deep inward gaze which opens the eyes of the soul to behold the presence of God, a man feels the steady rhythm of life itself. He seems to be behind the scene of all persons, things, and events. The deep hunger to be understood is at last seen to be one and the same with the hunger to understand.

Out of such an experience a new perspective emerges. Consciously now, the primary function or mission of life becomes that of achieving in act what one has experienced in insight. One is ever on the hunt for openings in others through which this may be achieved. Human need in all of its dimensions is the swinging door into the innermost life of another. To put it differently, it is the point at which the spirit is most highly sensitized for communication. If a man is moved from within his own spirit to do the deed of ministering to the need of another, and if the need of another is the point at which the spirit is most highly sensitized to communication, then it follows that the good deed is a meeting place for the mingling of one life with another. What a man has experienced in insight he achieves in the deed. What a difference giving makes now. It is no longer an offering merely of money or time or services, viewed as a sacrifice or a cause for merit, recognition, or glory. It is a simple sacrament, involving all of a person as his spirit moves through the swinging door of need into the very citadel of another's spirit.

26. Human Endurance

THERE often seems to be a clearly defined limit to human endurance. Everyone has had the experience of exhaustion. If you cannot get to bed you are sure that you will go to sleep standing. Then something happens. It may be that a friend comes by to see you, a friend whose path has not crossed yours in several years. It may be that there are tidings of good news or of tragedy. At any rate, something happens in you, with the result that you are awake, recovered, even excited. A few minutes before, the weariness was closing in like a dense fog. But now it is gone.

Of course, knowledge about the body and mind gives an increasingly satisfying explanation of this kind of experience. The important thing, however, is the fact that beyond the zero point of endurance there are vast possibilities. The precise limitations under which you live your particular life cannot be determined. Usually the stimulus, the incentive, must come from the outside—be brought to you on the wings of external circumstance. This means that the power available to you in great demand is not yours to command. I wonder!

This simple fact of revitalizing human endurance opens a great vista for living. It cannot be that what is possible to the body and nervous system by way of tapping the individual resource on demand is denied the spirit. The spirit in man is not easily vanquished. It is fragile *and* tough. You may fail again and again and yet something will not let you give up. Something keeps you from accepting "no"

44

as a final answer. It is this quality that makes for survival of values when the circumstances of one's life are most against decency, goodness, and right. Men tend to hold on when there seems to be no point in holding on, because they find that they *must*. It is often at such a point that the spirit in man and the spirit of God blend into one creative illumination. This is the great miracle. The body and the nervous system know.

27. The Miracle of Living

FREQUENTLY we are filled with a strange sense of the mystery and the miracle of life. In our private lives we are mindful of many blessings in a minor key, blessings so intimate, so closely binding, that they do not seem to be blessings at all:

> The ability to get tired and to be renewed by rest and relaxation; the whole range of tastes from sweet to bitter with the subtleties in between; the peculiar quality that cool water has for quenching the thirst; the color of sky and sea and the vast complex of hues that blend with objects, making the eye the inlet from rivers of movement and form; the sheer wonder of sound that gives to the inward parts feeling tones of the heights and the depths; the tender remembrance of moments that were good and whole, of places that reached out and claimed one as their very own, of persons who shared at depths beyond all measuring; the coming of day and the sureness of the return of the night, and all the dimensions of meaning that each of us finds in this cycle of movement which sustains and holds fast in the security of its rhythms. Thus, in our private lives, we are mindful of many blessings in a minor key.

Then there are the vast and lumbering awarenesses that live in us for which our hearts sing their joyful "amen":

> The land of our birth—the quality of climate that does not undermine the natural strength of body, the technique and skill

45

by which we are able to secure the windbreak against wind and storm, rain and heat; the fact and experience of family life where all the ingredients of the good life may first be made our own, against the time when we make our own way after the pattern of our own need for understanding.

Beyond all these there is the intimate sense of being upheld and cradled by strength that is not of our making, something that gives to life a quality of integrity and meaning which we, of ourselves, could never generate; the gentle upheaval in the heart reminding us to lift up our heads and be of good courage—

All of the benedictions of life flow in upon us, our Father— teach us how to make of our lives a Sacrament in Thy Hand, lest our spirits die and we vanish as shadows in the night. Amen.

28. Chains of Gold

"CHAINS of gold are no less chains than chains of iron."

This line is taken from one of the letters of Fénelon. He goes on to suggest that the person who is in chains is quite naturally the object of pity to anyone who is without chains. But the serious question is, Who is there that is without chains?

Chains are of various kinds and we need not be involved in the waste of equating them in terms of gold or iron. There are the chains that are ours because of the accidents of birth. It may be that if we had had a choice of parents we would have selected other parents. But would we? All that marked the lives of our parents before they were our parents may be directly reflected in how we were taught and in the atmosphere of our homes. These things influenced our lives deeply and in some strange way, perhaps, decided the limitations (chains) under which we live all our days.

There are the limitations owing to the experiences of our childhood beyond the ken of family and friends: the particular teacher in grade school whose life touched ours at a time and in a way that set in motion certain attitudes that can never quite leave us. These limitations sit in on all our subsequent decisions and leave the long trail of their consequences in everything we do.

There are habits which we formed at a time when we were scarcely aware that they were habits and what they would mean in the wide expanse of the years. They seemed so innocuous at the time—we did not know what they would be like when youth was far behind and all the full-blown demands of maturity would be upon us. These too are chains.

A little later in his letter Fénelon speaks of the comfort that comes from the realization that our chains may be fashioned by Providence. Here he is making no reference to fate or accident or tragedy but rather to the fact that one who is committed to God finds that he is no longer at liberty to do what he would be free to do if he were not so committed. He cannot hate another man even though to hate would be to pass on to another what would seem to be his just desert. He cannot throw his life away by living to no purpose because he is committed to follow a path which is His path wherever it takes him. ". . . After all, the consolation of knowing that you are where you are through God's Providence is quite inexhaustible; while you have that, nothing can matter. Well is it for those whom God cuts off from their own will, that they may follow Him."

29. The Night View of the World

"UPON the night view of the world, a day view must follow." This is an ancient insight grounded in the experience of the race in its long journey through all the years of man's becoming. Here is no cold idea born out of the vigil of some solitary thinker in lonely retreat from the traffic of the common ways. It is not the wisdom of the book put down in ordered words by the learned and the schooled. It is insight woven into the pattern of all living things, reaching its grand apotheosis in the reflection of man gazing deep into the heart of his own experience.

That the day view follows the night view is written large in nature. Indeed it is one with nature itself. The clouds gather heavy with unshed tears; at last they burst, sending over the total landscape waters

47

gathered from the silent offering of sea and river. The next day dawns and the whole heavens are aflame with the glorious brilliance of the sun. This is the way the rhythm moves. The fall of the year comes, then winter with its trees stripped of leaf and bud; cold winds ruthless in bitterness and sting. One day there is sleet and ice; in the silence of the nighttime the snow falls soundlessly—all this until at last the cold seems endless and all there is seems to be shadowy and foreboding. The earth is weary and heavy. Then something stirs—a strange new vitality pulses through everything. One can feel the pressure of some vast energy pushing, always pushing through dead branches, slumbering roots—life surges everywhere within and without. Spring has come. The day usurps the night view.

Is there any wonder that deeper than idea and concept is the insistent conviction that the night can never stay, that winter is ever moving toward the spring? Thus, when a man sees the lights go out one by one, when he sees the end of his days marked by death—his death—he *senses,* rather than knows, that even the night into which he is entering will be followed by day. It remains for religion to give this ancient wisdom phrase and symbol. For millions of men and women in many climes this phrase and this symbol are forever one with Jesus, the Prophet from Galilee. When the preacher says as a part of the last rites, "I am the Resurrection and the Life, . . ." he is reminding us all of the ancient wisdom: "Upon the night view of the world, a day view must follow."

30. Miracles in the Spirit

"THERE are miracles in the spirit of which the world knows nothing." Such is the testimony that comes to us from the lips of George Fox. Our lives are surrounded day by day and night after eventful night by the stupendous relevations of what man is discovering about the world around him. Each day we seem to penetrate more deeply into the process of nature. Thousands of men and women with utter devotion give themselves to the pursuit of secret disclosures from the chamber of mysteries of which they themselves are a part and from which they have come forth. It is as if there is a mighty collective and individual effort to remember what they were before the mind became mind and the body became flesh and blood. So successful has been the appropriation of the knowledge of the mysteries of air and wind and earth that what a decade ago would have startled and frightened the most matured adult is today taken for granted by the simplest child. We speak of going to the moon not as denizens of the shadows where unrealities tumble over one another in utter chaos. Rather we speak of going to the moon and back again with voices that are brimming over with an arrogance that even a god may not command.

But let one arise in our midst to speak of secrets of another kind. Let one say that the world of the spirit has vast frontiers which call to us as our native heath. At once the deep split in our spirits reveals itself. Out of our eyes, as we listen, there leaps the steady glow of recognition while our lips speak of superstition and delusion. Can the miracles in the spirit be real, true? Because they seem always to be personal and private, does this not add to their unreality?

The miracles in the spirit? What are they? The resolving of inner conflict upon which all the lances of the mind have splintered and fallen helplessly from the hand; the daring of the spirit that puts to rout the evil deed and the decadent unfaith; the experiencing of new purposes which give courage to the weak, hope to the despairing, life to those burdened by sin and failure; the quality of reverence that glows within the mind, illumining it with incentive to bring under the control of Spirit all the boundless fruits of knowledge; the necessity for inner and outer peace as the meaning of all men's striving; the discovery that the "Covenant of Brotherhood" is the witness of the work of the Spirit of God in the life of man and the hymn of praise offered to Him as Thanksgiving and Glory!

31. Joy Is of Many Kinds

JOY is of many kinds. Sometimes it comes silently, opening all closed doors and making itself at home in the desolate heart. It has no forerunner save itself; it brings its own welcome and salutation.

Sometimes joy is compounded of many elements: a touch of sadness, a whimper of pain, a harsh word tenderly held until all its arrogance dies, the casting of the eye into the face that understands, the clasp of a hand that holds, then releases, a murmur of tenderness where no word is spoken, the distilled moment of remembrance of a day, a night, an hour, lived beyond the sweep of the daily round—joy is often compounded of many things.

There is earned joy: an impossible job tackled and conquered, leaving no energy for assessing the price or measuring the cost, only an all-inclusive sense of well-being in the mind, and slowly creeping through all the crevices of the spirit—or it may be some dread has reared its head, gathering into itself all hope that is unassigned, until it becomes the master of the house, then relief comes through fresh knowledge, new insight, clearer vision. What was dread, now proves groundless and the heart takes to wings like an eagle in its flight.

There is the joy that is given. There are those who have in themselves the gift of Joy. It has no relation to merit or demerit. It is not a quality they have wrested from the vicissitudes of life. Such people have not fought and won a hard battle, they have made no conquest. To them Joy is given as a precious ingredient in life. Wherever they go, they give birth to Joy in others—they are the heavenly troubadours, earthbound, who spread their music all around and who sing their song without words and without sounds. To be touched by them is to be blessed of God. They give even as they have been given. Their presence is a benediction and a grace. In them we hear the music in the score and in their faces we sense a glory which is the very light of Heaven.

32. Always We Are Visited

How wonderful it is, beyond all power fully to understand, that our lives are never left to themselves alone. It does not matter where we are, nor what tasks consume our energies; there is always present something more than we ourselves are at any given moment. Always we are visited. Sometimes it is by an idea for which we do not seem to have had any previous preparation; sometimes by the penetration of an inspiration that shoots us out of the common path on to a road of high adventure; sometimes by the cumulative energy of a precious memory shedding a quiet haze over the entire landscape along which we walk. Sometimes we are called to do a hard job, before there is time to falter—a quickening of the pulse, a tightening of the mind, and away we go—always we are visited.

We are surrounded by the memory, the witness, and often the presence of those others, whose names we may or may not know, whose strivings make possible so much upon which we draw as a common heritage—those who carry the light against the darkness, those who stand up against tyranny even when to stand is not only idiotic but suicidal, those who forget themselves in the full response to something that calls them beyond the reaches of their dreams and their hopes.

We are surrounded by the testimony of those who, out of the life of the Spirit, speak directly to our spirit and to our need; those men and women with whom we identify in our moments of depression and despair and in our moments of joy and delight.

Therefore, our Father, we remember with gratitude to Thee all the springs of joy, renewal and recreation that are our common heritage and our common lot. We thank Thee for so great a gift and we offer to Thee our dedication and our response. Amen.

33. The Binding Unity

THERE is a unity that binds all living things into a single whole. This unity is sensed in many ways. Sometimes, when walking alone in the woods far from all the traffic which makes up the daily experience, the stillness settles in the mind. Nothing stirs. The imprisoned self seems to slip outside its boundaries and the ebb and flow of life is keenly felt. One becomes an indistinguishable part of a single rhythm, a single pulse.

Sometimes there is a moment of complete and utter identity with the pain of a loved one; all the intensity and anguish are *felt*. One enters through a single door of suffering into the misery of the whole human race with no margin left to mark the place which was one's own. What is felt belongs nowhere but is everywhere binding and holding in a tight circle of agony until all of life is gathered into a single timeless gasp!

There are other moments when one becomes aware of the thrust of a tingling joy that rises deep within until it bursts forth in radiating happiness that bathes all of life in its glory and its warmth. Pain, sorrow, grief, are seen as joy "becoming" and life gives a vote of confidence to itself, defining its meaning with a sureness that shatters every doubt concerning the broad free purpose of its goodness.

There are the times of personal encounter when a knowledge of caring binds two together and what is felt is good! There is nothing new nor old, only the knowledge that what comes as the flooding insight of love binds all living things into a single whole. The felt reverence spreads and deepens until to live and to love are to do *one* thing. To hate is to desire the nonexistence of the object of hate. To love is the act of adoration and praise shared with the Creator of life as the Be-all and the End-all of everything that is.

And yet there always remains the hard core of the self, blending and withdrawing, giving and pulling back, accepting and rejoicing, yielding and unyielding—what may this be but the pulsing of the unity that binds all living things in a single whole—the God of life extending Himself in the manifold glories of His creation?

34. Be Silent Together

"WE DO NOT know each other yet, we have not dared to be silent together." What a priceless possession is the gift of speech! To be able to make sounds convey specific meanings and deliberate notions, to be able to put at the disposal of another the feelings that nestle within the inner life, to be able to reveal one's self in symbols which make clear and do not betray—this is the miracle and the gift of the spoken word. It is with the word that man becomes human and thus makes possible the circles of relationships which make fast his sense of self. It is the word that gives him the power to hurt where no panacea can touch, to harness the wild horses of the mind and make them the burden bearers of the heart, to give wings to earthbound values until they lose themselves on far horizons—it is the word that can create or destroy, splinter or make whole, redeem or damn.

It is small wonder that man tends to worship the sound of his voice and to give to it an authority greater than anything that remains when all words have been said. If he can put together the words of conveyance, then he thinks that communication has fulfilled itself. Silence is not trusted; it is subversive; it must be hidden. Fear of silence is the offering which we place upon the altar of words. This is in part due to the richness of the experience of speech, and we do not wish to let it escape from us lest we descend once again into the vast empty region where there are no words, where there is no speech.

It is important to remember that it is out of the silence that all sounds come; it is in the stillness that the word is fashioned for the meaning it conveys. Here the sound without sounds can be most clearly heard and meanings out of which all values come can be plumbed. Thus Maeterlinck writes, "If it be indeed your desire to give yourself over to another, be silent. . . . Some there are that have no silence, and that kill the silence around them, and these are the only creatures that pass through life unperceived. To them it is not given to cross the zone of revelation, the great zone of firm and faithful light. We cannot conceive what sort of man is he who has never been silent. It is to us as though his soul were featureless. 'We do not know each other yet . . . we have not yet dared to be silent together.' "

35. . . . Paths We Did Not Know

"He leads us on by paths we did not know."

There is an abiding desire to know the future, to see around the corner of the days and years. Even when we say we do not concern ourselves about what will happen next month or next year, the shy insistence still remains—we want to know.

This normal feeling is a part of all the anxiety which we face on the threshold of any new adventure. If we could be sure that all will be well—if we could have some guarantee that our present hopes would not betray us and leave us deserted in the lonely place—then we would find the peace that belongs to the contented.

But life is not like that. The future is never quite a thing apart from all that has gone before. We bring into the present ingredients and cargoes from the past, and these are with us as we take the unknown road. All that we have learned, felt, and thought, all our experience from birth to now; all the love that nourished us at other times, all the yearnings rooted in our spirits—all these are with us as we move into the unknown way.

And then, there is the witness of others who have gone along the road we take. True, the road will mean for us something unique but not altogether unique. The generations meet and share, in ways beyond our grasp, the secrets of the new path, the first step, the beginning way.

"He leads us on by paths we did not know."

36. Not by Bread Alone

THE spirit swept upon him
Like some winged creature from above!
Light was all around:
　Every leaf shimmered and danced,
　A swirling dervish in a timeless trance.
The sky was lost in light.
He saw and felt the light.

From all around, here, there, everywhere
The Voice whispered in tones that sang:
　"Thou art my son; this day I claim you as my own . . ."
Wrapped in the echo of the sound
He took the way beyond the city gates,
Beyond the crooked path
Where the rocks began!
He walked until wilderness, rocky ledge and quiet
Were all around. He found a resting place to wait.

When the burning cooled and his mind would ease,
    Then he would know.

Time passed making no sound and there was none to count the hour.

Into his mind one question came:
    What is man's life?
    Is it for bread he strives
    That dreams might last?
There is a way to hold the gate
'Gainst hunger as a common fate:
Make bread the all-absorbing aim,
And give to it a prior claim.
There would be space for inner things
For the heavy fruit of prophet's dream.
It seemed so clear what he must do.
Lost in the labyrinth of Fancy's ways,
He had not reckoned with the Voice:
    "No, not by bread alone."
It leaped into his mind like a thing possessed!
    "No, not by bread alone."
The hills picked up the words and gave them sound;
Tramped the rhythm on wind and cloud, in sky and air,
All around, everywhere:
    "No, not by bread alone.
    Man does not live by bread alone.
Out of the mouth of God
All good things come:
Truth and beauty; goodness, love—.
    No, not by bread alone."

37. Thou Shalt Not Tempt God

HE WAS scarcely awake;
He was not quite asleep.
His mind ranged over the whole expanse of all his years

Until it came to rest on the fateful day beside the Jordan.
He felt again the pounding of his heart,
The quickening of his spirit
When his eyes were caught by the stare of John
Whose flaming words had found their mark.
> God had held him in his mother's womb,
> Had pursued him with His great Command!
> Each day brought something more beside itself
> Spilling over from another realm.
> There was a hint of caution choking the careless word.
> There were ancient hungers held at bay lest the way be lost.

Then there was his mother.
> At work, at play; always in her eyes the haunting fear,
> Gentled by the searching love of her brooding heart.
> Each step took him farther than her hopes could reach.

He remembered words plunging from his startled lips
While Temple men looked on in wonder and were brought to tears.

> "Suppose," he thought, "suppose there were no boundaries
>   by which my life were set.
> The common laws of creatures set aside,
> I could thwart the orders holding all of life?
> Then would I firm the claim that I am God's son!
> Who then could make a counterclaim?
> I could reign supreme in my father's stead.
> Then what of Him? . .

> How long the soundless words had filled my mind
>   I do not know.
> At last they found their voice:

>> 'Thou shalt not tempt God!
>> Thou shalt not tempt God
>> To destroy His son.' "

38. Thou Shalt Worship God

HE HAD wondered about the hill above the rock
    on which he sat.
In and out of his mind the query came.
A little while before the sun was lost
    beyond the hill
He stirred himself to move.
At the top of the hill he stood transfixed:
    The sun nestled on the edge of a cloud at bay—
    A soft iridescence blanketed all the air above, below.

    To the East the clouds were alive with many forms:
        Chariots, horsemen, and marching legions,
        Men and women in ceaseless motion
        Filling a thousand market squares with mild commotion.
    And high above, disappearing in the heavens
    Huge columns resting on the vast panorama
    As on a living throne:
        The Kingdoms of this world—

    Jesus looked and trembled.

Darkness crept down; the stars returned.
Slowly he started back along the path.
The kingdoms of this world . . .
"What if I could . . . Oh, No!
Suppose I could. It is too fantastic.
If I could bring it off:
All their force and power
An instrument for good.
By mighty acts which none could brook
Fear and hunger would disappear.
The deeds of peace would banish plans for war.

57

Such is my Father's will.
But how could these things be?
If all the God in me could serve the world,
Kings, kingdoms, earthly rulers all
Would disappear.
And in their place the Mind of God would sit enthroned.
His son would rule for Him.
The praise due Him and Him alone would come to me . . .

I heard the Voice, His Voice."

Thou shalt worship God alone
And Him only shalt thou serve.

39. "My God! My God! . . ."

HE WAS dying!
Jesus had come to the cross by a direct path!
Despite the agony of all the pain
There was the sense of pure relief
That he and the dogging shadow were face to face!
Nothing could reach him now.
He was beyond the violence of all his foes,
He thought.
He gripped the pain!
He established its place and bade it stay!
Death was at hand, he knew:
A zone of peace holds fast the place
Where pain and death are met.
Pinnacled on its lonely height, he waited.
Then came the crash of words:
    "Come down! Come down!
    If you believe your words,
    Call the angels to do their work."
    "If you are God's son, make good your claim!
    Come down! Come down! Come down!"

His spirit quaked! His mind tilted.
The pain escaped; his whole world shifted!
   "My God! My God! Hast Thou forsaken me?"
The words leaped forth!

He wondered had he missed the way.
Could it be true that he was sure of God
But God not sure of him?
The day at the Jordan his mind recalled;
Into the desert wilderness he sought the clue.
The mount with Moses and Elijah came to mind.
He remembered the Cup
And the long night beneath the olive trees.
   "This is the Cup; not Death!
   To yield the right to prove the Truth
   As if it could not stand alone.
   This is the Cup; not Death!
   Father, into Thy Hands, I give my life."

The Quest for Fulfillment

It takes time to cultivate the mind.
It takes time to grow in wisdom.

40. The Daily Tempest

IT IS a commonplace remark that our lives are surrounded with so much movement, so many pressures, so many demands, that our spirits are often crowded into a corner. As soon as we awaken in the morning we are taken over by the ruthlessness of our daily routine. In some important ways this is good. It means that there is a regularity and a structure to our days that make it possible for us to accomplish tasks which would be impossible otherwise.

But there is another aspect of the matter of daily time tables—an oppressive aspect. We are made prisoner by time tables. We become busy—note the words: not, we are busy, but we *become* busy. Within ourselves we develop an inner sense of *rush* and *haste*. There is a kind of anxiety that is like the sense of impending doom that comes into the life when the spirit is crowded by too much movement.

It is true that for many people the demands upon their lives are so great that only careful planning in terms of a workable time table can see them through. Even where the demands are not great and overwhelming, the economy, the efficiency of an established way of functioning, is undeniable. The purpose of such a pattern is not merely to accomplish more work and with dispatch, but it is to increase the margin of one's self that is available for the cultivation of the inner life. It takes time to cultivate the mind. It takes time to grow in wisdom. It takes time to savor the qualities of living. It takes time to feel one's way into one's self. It takes time to walk with God.

Forsake us not in the tempests of our daily activities, O our Father, but tutor our minds and spirits in the great tranquilities, that deep within we may be still and know that Thou art God. Amen.

41. Freedom Is a Discipline

THERE is a medley of confusion as to the meaning of personal freedom. For some it means to function without limitations at any point, to be able to do what one wants to do and without hindrance. This is the fantasy of many minds, particularly those that are young. For others, personal freedom is to be let alone, to be protected against any force that may move into the life with a swift and decisive imperative. For still others, it means to be limited in one's power over others only by one's own strength, energy, and perseverance.

The meaning of personal freedom is found in none of these. They lack the precious ingredient, the core of discipline and inner structure without which personal freedom is delusion. At the very center of personal freedom is a discipline of the mind and of the emotions. The mind must be centered upon a goal, a purpose, a plan. Of all possible goals, purposes, plans, a single one is lifted above the others and held as one's chosen direction. Then the individual knows when he is lost, when he has missed the way. There emerges a principle of orderedness which becomes a guide for behavior and action. Under such circumstances, goals may be changed deliberately and the sense of random, pointless living is removed.

Such a principle of orderedness provides a channel for one's emotions and drive. Energy is no longer dissipated but it is used to supply dynamic for the pursuit of the end. Here we come upon the most interesting aspect of personal freedom—the living of one's life with confidence that transcends discouragement and despair. This means that one does not have to depend upon the favorable circumstance, the fortuitous "break," the applause, approval, and felicitation of friends, important as these are. The secret is the quiet inner purpose and the release of vitality with which it inspires the act. Achieving the goal is not measured by some external standard, though such must not be completely ignored. Rather, it is measured in terms of loyalty to the purpose and the freedom which it inspires.

"Seek ye first the rule of God," the Master says. And after that? The key that one needs for one's peace is in the heart. There can be no personal freedom where there is not an initial personal surrender.

42. Results Not Crucial

IN ONE of the parables Jesus tells the story of a certain nobleman who went abroad to obtain power for himself and then return. Before he left he called his ten servants, giving them each a twenty-dollar bill, and telling them, "Trade with this until I come back." When he returned, he ordered his servants to be brought before him for their report.

The first man said, "Sir, your twenty dollars have made one hundred."

"Fine," said the nobleman.

The second man said, "Sir, your twenty dollars have made fifty dollars."

"Excellent," said the nobleman.

The third man was the only one who made a speech. He said, "Sir, here is your twenty dollars. I kept it safe in a napkin, for I was afraid of you. Perhaps you do not know this, but you have a reputation of being a very hard man. You pick up what you have never put down. You reap where you have not sown, you gather into barns what you have not planted!"

The nobleman was incensed. He ordered the servant cast off his place into "outer darkness."

Here, I make an end of the story. The unfortunate servant was not "cast off" because he did not realize any profit for the nobleman. No. He was cast off because he did not "work at it."

We are never under obligation to achieve results. Of course, results are important and it may be that that is the reason effort is put forth. But results are not mandatory. Much of the energy and effort and many anxious hours are spent over the probable failure or success of our ventures. No man likes to fail. But it is important to remember that under certain circumstances, failure is its own success.

To keep one's eye on results is to detract markedly from the business at hand. This is to be diverted from the task itself. It is to be only partially available to demands at hand. Very often it causes one to betray one's own inner sense of values because to hold fast to the integrity of the act may create the kind of displeasure which in the end will affect the results. However, if the results are left free to form themselves in terms of the quality and character of the act, then all of one's resources can be put at the disposal of the act itself.

There are many forces over which the individual can exercise no control whatsoever. A man plants a seed in the ground and the seed sprouts and grows. The weather, the winds, the elements, cannot be controlled by the farmer. The result is never a sure thing. So what does the farmer do? He plants. Always he plants. Again and again he works at it—the ultimate confidence and assurance that even though his seed does not grow to fruition, seeds do grow and they do come to fruition.

The task of men who work for the Kingdom of God, is to *Work* for the Kingdom of God. The result beyond this demand is not in their hands. He who keeps his eyes on results cannot give himself wholeheartedly to his task, however simple or complex that task may be.

43. Do Your Own Thinking

IT WAS a class in plane geometry. All through the term I had great difficulty in trying to find a way to master the materials. I studied long and hard, seeking help from anyone who seemed to have an ability greater than mine. Slowly the tide turned in my favor until it began flowing full and free. You can imagine my transport when the unbelievable miracle took place: There came a day when the entire class was "stumped" by a theorem that I could work. I raised my hand, shook my fingers, doing everything except calling the teacher's name. At last he called on me but not before he had reached my name in alphabethical order. I recited with a flourish. It was obvious to everyone but me that I was beside myself with arrogance.

When I finished there was an active silence while I waited for the congratulations due me, as I thought. After all, none of the others knew the answer and I did. This in itself was worthy of felicitation. At length the teacher spoke: "Will Howard Thurman stop by my desk when the bell rings." He did not make it a personal remark. It was more like an announcement over a public-address system. I could hardly wait. In fact, I was hardly aware of what transpired during the rest of the period. When the bell rang, I busied myself at my seat because I did not want anyone to enjoy my moment of triumph with me. I was sure that the teacher was going to tell me that I had the makings of a great creative mathematician. The classroom emptied itself; only I was left alone with the teacher. I stood before his desk, waiting.

"Howard," he said, "you must always do your own thinking but remember Wisdom was not born with you. That is all." In these nineteen words there was held before me a mirror. What I saw I have never quite forgotten.

It is easy to create the illusion that knowledge in one little area gives one authority in many other or in all areas. A man becomes an expert swimmer, or a specialist in some particular field of human knowledge, and the assumption tends to develop that he knows much about many other areas of knowledge. The Greeks were aware of this pitfall. They used the happy phrase "as to" whenever they were passing judgment on a man's knowledge or wisdom. Such a man was great "as to" some particular thing. This made for humility and a peculiar kind of reverence for the truth.

Sometimes children are tempted to think that because they have advantages of training and opportunities for development that were denied their parents, they are wise and their parents foolish. Sometimes a man is visited by the Spirit of God which results in such a renewal of life that he is tempted to turn his insight into bigotry and his religious experience into a spiritual pride. Sometimes it is very hard not to pray: "O God, I thank Thee that I am not as other men." Knowledge of fact may inspire pride and arrogance; wisdom makes for understanding and humility.

> State the tides and regulate the sun
> Then drop into thyself and be a fool.

44. Saddle Your Dreams

"SADDLE your dreams before you ride them." It is the nature of dreams to run riot, never to wish to contain themselves within limitations that are fixed. Sometimes they seem to be the cry of the heart for the boundless and the unexplored. Often they are fashioned out of longings too vital to die, out of hankerings fed by hidden springs in the dark places of the spirit. Often they are the offspring of hopes that can never be realized and longings that can never find fulfillment. Sometimes they are the weird stirrings of ghosts of dead plans and the kindling of ashes in a hearth that has long since been deserted. Many and fancy are the names by which dreams are called—fantasies, repressed desires, vanities of the spirit, will-o'-the-wisps. Sometimes we seek to dismiss them by calling their indulgence daydreaming, by which we mean, taking flight from the realities of our own world and dwelling in the twilight of vain imaginings.

All of this may be true. But all their meaning need not be exhausted by such harsh judgment. The dreams belong to us; they come full-blown out of the real world in which we work and hope and carry on. They are not imposters. They are not foreign elements invading our world like some solitary comet from the outer reaches of space which pays one visit to the sun and is gone never to come again. No! Our dreams are our *thing.* They become *other* when we let them lose their character. Here is the fatal blunder. Our dreams must be saddled by the hard facts of our world before we ride them off among the stars. Thus, they become for us the bearers of the new possibility, the enlarged horizon, the great hope. Even as they romp among the stars they come back to their place in our lives, bringing with them the radiance of the far heights, the lofty regions, and giving to all our days the lift and the magic of the stars.

45. The Idea and the Reality

> Between the idea
> And the reality
> Between the motion
> And the act
> Falls the shadow.*

THIS QUOTATION from T. S. Eliot's "The Hollow Men" puts into crisp words one of the oldest problems of the human spirit. There is always the riding frustration to all human effort that makes it fall short of the intent, the clear-cut purpose. Sometimes it is very difficult for the idea or the plan to be clearly defined. It is hard to make up one's mind about goals because motives are often confused. To know precisely what it is that we want is often a very torturous process.

And yet, the great frustration is not at the point of the elusive and indefinable goal or purpose. It is rather at the point of determining how to span the gulf that lies between the goal and its fulfillment, the purpose and its realization. The gulf is deep and wide between the dream and the implementation. Look at any achievement of your life, however simple or elaborate! There is one judgment that you can pass upon it: it is so much less than you had in mind. As the dream lay nestled in your mind untouched by the things that sully or corrupt, you were stirred to the deep places within by its rightness, by its beauty, by its truth. Then the time of birth was upon you—the dream took its place among the stuff of your daily round. Looking upon it now, it is so much less than what it seemed to be before. It is ever thus.

A man sees the good and tries to achieve it in what he thinks, says, and does. With what results? You know your answer. How often have you felt: the good I see I do not, or the good I see I achieve only in such limited, inadequate ways that I wonder even about the vision

---

* "The Hollow Men" in *Collected Poems 1909-1935* by T. S. Eliot (New York: Harcourt, Brace & World, Inc., 1936).

itself. Always there is the shadow. Always there is the wide place between the dream and its fulfillment.

46. Let Not Thy Will Be Set to Sin

"LET NOT thy will be set to sin." These searching words are from the Book of Tobit. The attitude toward wrongdoing depends upon the character of the individual conscience. Conscience is rooted in the sense of value which is a part of the working equipment of personality. This sense of value is given; but the content varies. Here the results of training, observation, social heritage, or religious experience and instruction are made manifest. The judgment which says that a deed is wrong is always a reflection of the content of the individual's sense of value. So often such a judgment concerning wrongdoing does not involve the will of the individual. There seems to be an automatic, unreflective element in conscience. A man says, "I do not know why this is wrong; all that I know is, this is the way I feel about it." Or he may say, "I know my feeling of guilt for what I have done does not make sense, except to me."

Again and again we find ourselves reacting to events and situations apart from our will in the matter. Our reaction is the way we are trained, conditioned, taught. But this does not alter the fact of our responsibility for our acts and reactions. An important part of living is the process by which the individual *will* brings under its private jurisdiction the behavior of the individual. This is an essential element in any doctrine of self-mastery, or, more accurately, of self-knowledge.

How many things have we done during the past week for which we have an after-the-event sense of responsibility, reflected in guilt, hostility, or pride? Deeds which did not express our conscious intent because the doing of the deeds did not come before our will for review. The action was automatic, the result of long-established habits, training, conditioning. But once the deed was done and we were faced with the consequences, we realized that this kind of behavior was not our intent. The common cry is: I did not know. I did not understand.

It is important to make the full conquest of one's life pattern to the end that one's deeds will flow more and more from the center of one's intent. Perhaps this is a goal that is never reached, but to work at it is to become increasingly mature and responsible. Meditation and prayer are helpful in providing a climate in which one's deeds may be exposed and the character of the deeds understood. In such a climate, the most natural desire of the heart is the quiet utterance to God:

> Let not my will be set to sin.

47. Not Daunted by an Interval

> I will not be daunted
> By an interval.

To EXPERIENCE physical pain and/or its equivalent is to suffer. In suffering there is always a margin of freedom for the movement of the mind and the emotions away from the core of the suffering. It is for this reason that many people who suffer find their creativity intensified, their powers greatly enhanced.

To experience personal despair owing to some weakness in one's own character is tragedy. In tragedy, the individual stands on the brink of fulfillment, comes within reach of the city of his dreams; something happens, something goes wrong, there is the crucial moment, and the precise ingredient needed is not there.

To experience the sense of utter isolation, to feel one's self cut off from all resources, left to one's self alone, is to be afflicted. In affliction the individual seems to himself to be deserted not merely by man but by God. It is this last that grips the soul with a frozen agony in which the final iota of energy is consumed by an anguished cry.

Much of the drama of the week of the Passion as observed by the Christian world has to do with the experience of the central Figure of our faith with suffering, the sense of tragedy, and the intense convulsion of affliction. The pain of the cross and the wrenching of the mind and spirit from its intensity; the heavy cry that the cup might pass, when his whole life was threatened with tragedy; the desolation that forced from blistered lips the ancient wail of the Psalmist, "My God, my God, why hast thou forsaken me"—these were the forms that the drama took.

But deep within the center of the turbulent sequences there stirred something else, in response to an insistence in Jesus, that moved into him straight from the Heart of God. The words of the opening quotation find their meaning now—

I will not be daunted
By an interval.

The power that enables a person to resist the terrible necessity for scaling down his faith, his hopes, his dreams, his commitment, to the level of the event which is his immediate experience—this is finally the meaning of the triumph of life over death, of strength over weakness, of joy over sorrow, of love over hate. This is the power of the Resurrection, which is rooted in the life of God, available to all men in every age, in every faith, everywhere.

48. Lest Your Activity Consume You

"I AM AFRAID lest your natural activity should consume you amid the painful circumstances which surround you."

In this sentence Fénelon calls attention to one of the persistent problems of inner growth. We are surrounded by what is quaintly called "natural" activities. The daily round is made up of such activities. There is the simple business of preparing for the day; waking up, dressing, getting breakfast and doing all the little things incidental to getting at the day's demands. For each new day there are myriad things that are carried over from the preceding day. Then there are the regularly scheduled activities that belong to a specific day. Some things must be done today, for instance, because today is Tuesday; there are Wednesday "things," Thursday "things," and so on for each succeeding day through the week. These are in the nature of routine commitments by virtue of what our total undertakings are and what our immediate goals happen to be.

In addition to these there are those "natural" activities that fall within the category of the casual, the inconsequential. By strict accounting they may be regarded as "fooling around," doing nothing in particular—a form of social doodling. It is here that we become involved in much waste of time and energy. As we look back upon the week we see that at staggered intervals during any day we have idled away precious minutes or hours with nothing to validate their expenditure. The use of such time can be important if it is to catch one's breath or to take a respite from pressures.

The important thing to hold in mind is that all of our energies must not be consumed in merely getting through the day or the week. In the living of our lives from day to day we must be geared to goals or purposes that inform the character of all our activities. Our living must be structured by what it is that we are trying to achieve with our lives. Without seeming melodramatic, it is urgent to say that for many, the days which they are living now are all the days they will have. The only contribution that they will make to the total of man's living and striving is being made now. What will be the extent of a man's life he does not know—in what time or place he will come to an end is not given to him to know. The wise man, therefore, lives his life seriously each day but he does not take it seriously.

49. Squads of Emotions

THERE is an unforgettable line in T. S. Eliot's *Four Quartets:* "Undisciplined squads of emotions." There is much talk about the meaning of human relations and the necessity for deepening the kind and quality of understanding among men. The notion is widespread among us that good will can be left to manage itself in the affairs of men. Thinking along this line leads to chaos and confusion. Left to itself good will depreciates into "undisciplined squads of emotions." A man has an inflamed appendix; in due course nature will rupture it; surgery in that instance would be unnecessary. But the result is apt to be peritonitis. There is always the necessity to put a hard idea at the core of the emotion or else the result may be fatal as well as reckless.

A man is ill. Those who love him may, out of the tenderness of their feelings, administer to him without any understanding of his malady and thereby hasten his end. There is a discipline of mind, of plan, of procedure, of skill, of technique, necessary to the wise and creative function of the emotions. Where this does not obtain the good feeling may become a monstrous thing destructive of all values which it intends to preserve.

Good will must be worked at, must be used as energy to carry out the thoughtful plan and the sound idea. It is a searching question— How much of my own kindly feeling toward another is unfocused and unintelligent? or How much do I understand the person for whom I have the good feeling, the warm heart? A man must study how to be effective in expressing the good which his moral concern inspires. This must be done without self-consciousness or calculation. The good will must remain spontaneous even while it is guided and directed to accomplish its highest ends. The seeming paradox can be resolved only in the living experience of one who has learned *to feel* with wisdom and to love with understanding.

"Undisciplined squads of emotions" must become a part of the power of the personality as it fulfills itself in devotion to friend and foe. The mind must be clear and precise while the heart continues warm and urgent. In so personal and grand an undertaking the man of good will has at his constant disposal the strength of God whose way with men is constant in its firmness and unyielding in its tenderness.

50. To Rise to the Great Occasion

IT IS NOT too difficult to rise to the great occasion, to put forth the tremendous effort for the great moment. Again and again men find it possible to withstand the great temptation, to measure up to the formidable enemy who threatens or challenges.

The radical test for life seems to be most actively at work in the experience in which the stakes are highest and most exacting. This is always a part of the appeal of war. When the nation is threatened, then every man becomes important in a new way. He may not have counted before but at a time of national peril the total welfare becomes an insistent part of his responsibility. Have you ever been in a regional or city disaster caused by flood, earthquake, or fire? At such a time everybody becomes involved—the ne'er-do-well, the people beyond the tracks, the rich, the poor, the good, the bad. This is the moment of judgment and all must be present and accounted for.

But the most searching graces of life are made up of the "tiny nothings." The pulse of the daily round that keeps the living process on its way is the source of the sustaining quality of all of life. One of the strengths of character is the ability to stand fast at the level of the commonplace and the ordinary. When the big temptation has failed to destroy a man, he may succumb to the relentless pressure of the "tiny nothings" that will not let him be.

It is at the point of the "tiny nothings" that human relations break down when they seem most secure. The thousand little things which in themselves can never be pinpointed, the petty annoyances that puncture the rhythm of creative, daily companionship, the little word expressing the big meaning—these are the walls that rise quietly in the nighttime, shutting one man away from his fellows.

Our Father, greatly increase the quality of our awareness of the little processes which make up the daily round of our living. Tenderize all the hard places in our emotions that we may be alive to Thy Spirit in the simplest exposures of the daily round. Amen.

51. A Life at Cross-Purposes

THERE is nothing more exhausting for the person than the constant awareness that his life is being lived at cross-purposes. At such moments the individual seems to himself ever to be working against himself. What he longs for is the energy that comes from a concentration of his forces in a single direction, toward a single end. Often this is impossible of achievement because of many factors. It may be that a person has so many gifts of such high order that the pull in many directions is authentic and convincing. It may be that the goal that beckons is one requiring the kind of preparation that is impossible of fulfillment because of circumstances that will not yield to the intent, however compelling the intent may be. Perhaps what the dream is set upon offers no precedent in his own story, thereby rendering null and void the confidence, even the effort. Or it may be that a man has turned his back upon the vision that gripped him and accepted in its place something that fell within the easy reach of untaxed powers.

There is still another dimension in which a man may be a victim of cross-purposes. He may be set in his life's commitment with a personal equipment and discipline equal to his choice; but he feels under pressure to include in his activity additional duties that are compelling in themselves but are apart from the meaning of his commitment. At such a time a decision must be reached that will enable him to say: This one thing I do—this one way I take—this one commitment I honor. To take such a stand may mean being bitterly judged and grossly misinterpreted—it may mean a loss of prestige and a shattering of ties that bind into the lives of many others. There is always the possibility that he may be mistaken—the victim of pride, arrogance, and conceit. Lurking ever in the background is the threat that one has taken the easier way out; one is doing the convenient and less costly thing.

At long last the only redemption from the paralysis of the cross-purpose is to seek with all possible intent to link one's deepest desire with one's choice of goal and to make of one's life a dedication to such an end. Ultimately a man's responsibility is to God; the God a man worships is the God he must face. And when he stands before Him, what shall he say?

52. To Be Free from Care

THERE is natural longing for a life that is free from carking care. The important thing is not that we want to live in the empty monotony of sameness but that what we want is to be relieved of the pressure of anxiety that comes from finding no escape from the things that make life hard. There is an insistent urgency of the unpleasant task or the handicap of mind or body that clings within our enthusiasm and seems ever abiding. For many there is the fear that a disease that has been put to flight will return in full force, laying waste the body and despoiling all the dreams of a lifetime. In fine we want to be rid of the things that encumber, that make more difficult the journey which is set before us. . . . Persistent anxieties, time-wearied weaknesses, uncontrollable and explosive tempers; scar tissues from old injuries, the troubled feeling that we can never quite define owing to our intimate reaction to the impact of the age of violence in which we live . . .

In our times of quiet, of meditation, either alone or in the midst of the congregation, we come to grips with what to us is our tragic fact, our private predicament. Patiently we seek to detach ourselves and take a long look in two dimensions—one at our lives free of our burden; the other, at our lives underneath our load. It is then that we give wings to our longings. As we wait in the silence, sometimes clearly, sometimes feebly, an answer comes.

With fumbling words we give ourselves to prayer:

> Our Father, we want to be rid of that which comes between us and Thy vision. Teach us how. We are but little children stumbling in the darkness. Do not reject even our weakness, O God, but accept us totally as we are. Work over us, knead us and fashion us until at last we take on the character which is Thy Spirit and the mind which is Thy Mind. We trust Thee to do Thy Things in us, O God, God the Father of our spirits. Amen.

53. Your Neighbor's Landmarks

"THINK twice before you move your neighbor's landmarks."

There is an ancient wisdom in this timely caution. Curious indeed is the form of arrogance that causes a man to feel that it is his peculiar right to set the whole world in order—to close all open things—to make all crooked paths straight. Such an attitude says that all knowledge, all virtue, all truth, can be contained in a single vessel. This is a great sacrilege.

It is important to remember that one man is never quite in a position to see what it is that another man sees. What one man may never know is precisely how an event, an act, or a thing is experienced by another man. We are uninformed about the content that a man brings to the events of his life. We do not know what was at work in a man when he staked his claim on an aspect of life.

In the long way that we take, in our growing up, in the vicissitudes of life by which we are led into its meaning and its mystery, there are established for us, for each one of us, certain landmarks. They represent discoveries sometimes symbolizing the moment when we became aware of the purpose of our lives; they may establish for us our membership in the human frailty; they may be certain words that were spoken into a stillness within us the sound thereof singing forever through all the corridors of our being as landmarks; yes, each one of us has his own. No communication between people is possible if there is not some mutual recognition of the landmarks. There are no reverences that bind us together as people that can be meaningful if the landmarks are profaned. To understand a man is not merely to know his name and the number of his thoughts, to be acquainted with how he acts or what he does. To know a man is to know, somewhat, of his landmarks. For these are his points of referral that stand out beyond and above all the traffic of his life, advising and tutoring him in his journey through life and beyond. In the language of religion, these are the places where the Eternal has been caught and held for a swirling moment in time and years. "Think twice before you move your neighbor's landmarks."

54. No Life Without War and Affliction

"FOR whatsoever plans I shall devise for my own peace, my life cannot be without war and affliction."

It is natural to have a plan for one's life. The mind is always trying to make sense out of experience. This is true even when there does not seem to be a pattern or plan on the basis of which an individual lives his life. There are some people who by temperament are so orderly that no action is contemplated by them in the absence of a well-defined plan. If such a person is making a simple journey, careful attention is given to every detail of schedule and of events in which he is likely to be involved. For him each day is ordered between the hours of waking and of sleeping.

There are others for whom planning comes hard. They put off every detail until the last minute and move through life in a kind of breathless confusion. They depend upon chance and the particular circumstance to determine what must or must not be done. There is a sense in which their lives are lived in a state of extended crisis.

But whether one falls into one or the other category or somewhere in between, there is a sense in which one's life moves within the structure of pattern and plan. Particularly is this true of one's life as a whole. There are things that one finds meaningful and things that one likes or dislikes. There are goals that are kept before one— vocation, personal fulfillment in family life, status, position, prestige. In such contemplation of goals, there is a normal tendency to exclude the things that would make for conflict and turmoil and to include the things that will make for peace and tranquillity.

Thomas à Kempis reminds us that it is the nature of life and man's experience in it, that there be what he calls "war and affliction." This is not a note of pessimism and futility—it is rather a recognition that conflict is a part of the life process. Whatever may be the plan which one has for one's life, one must *win* the right to achieve it. Again and again in the struggle a man may experience failure but he must know for himself that even though such is his experience, the final word has not been spoken. Included in his plan must be not only the possibility of failure but also the fact that he will not escape struggle, conflict, and war. Mr. Valiant-for-Truth in *Pilgrim's Progress* says, "My sword I give to him that shall succeed me in my pilgrimage, and my courage and skill to him that can get it. My marks and my scars I carry with me, to be a witness for me that I have fought His battle who will be my rewarder."

55. The Subtleties of Pride

IT IS GOOD to be reminded of the subtleties of pride. There is the pride of the private life—the moods which tempt us to think more highly of ourselves than we ought to think. Perhaps they are more than moods. It may well be that what was once a mood, or a temporary device to help one over a rough place in the private journey, has settled into an established pattern of thought and attitude. The peril in thinking more highly of one's self than one ought to think is the effect that it has on the ability to live effectively within one's limitations. It blinds the inner eye and dulls the judgment. It exposes the individual to frustration and futility. It breeds arrogance and conceit while undermining the gentle grace of humility. There is a kind of boastfulness in effort even though there is no word uttered. Very often the way in which a thing is done says more than a thousand words. Humility is not merely an attitude; it manifests itself also in the quality of the deed.

The Master gives a graphic picture of pride in the private life. He tells of two men who went up into the Temple to pray. One man announced himself to God, saying his gratitude because he was not as other men. He was good while other men were bad. He paid his vows while others did not. He prayed several times a day while others did not. The picture is very vividly drawn: pride, arrogance, conceit, even before God. The other man—what about him? He did not lift his voice aloud. He did not even lift up his face as he muttered, "God, have mercy upon me, a sinner."

One of the results of the prideful attitude is the effect of the reaction of other people. They do not wish him well—they are apt to be glad when he fails and to restrain even the good impulse to lend a hand. They surround him with an atmosphere of nonsupport which closes the doors one by one until isolation is precise and effective. It is a *desolate* way when there is none to wish him well and to cheer him along *his* way.

If a person thinks more highly of himself than he ought to think, he can never know what is perhaps the most important truth: the truth about himself.

Teach me, O God, how to walk humbly before Thee that not by work, not by deed, not by thought, will I do violence to the confidence and trust of those who walk the way with me. Cradle me in humility that I may be worthy of the simplest gesture of friendliness even from the stranger whose name I may never know. Amen.

56. The Decision to Act

IT IS a wondrous thing that a decision to act releases energy in the personality. For days on end a person may drift along without much energy, having no particular sense of direction and having no will to change. Then something happens to alter the pattern. It may be something very simple and inconsequential in itself but it stabs awake, it alarms, it disturbs. In a flash one gets a vivid picture of one's self—and it passes. The result is decision, sharp, definitive decision. In the wake of the decision, yes, even as a part of the decision itself, energy is released. The act of decision sweeps all before it and the life of the individual may be changed forever.

In the act the individual has a sense of personal stake. Once the decision is made all other options are frozen and in their place is compulsion. There is something so irrevocable about the act—perhaps that is why the tendency to dally and to postpone is ever present. A man may be sorry for the act, he may wish that he could undo it, he may long for the wheels of time to reverse themselves so that he could start again. He may try to redeem the act by some other act which counteracts what he has done. He may do all of these things, but he cannot alter the finality of the act itself.

It is good that this is so, for it means that the integrity of the act is private, personal, inescapable. Whatever may be the pressure to which a person yields, whatever may be the fears and anxieties which push him to the point of decision from which his act flows, whatever may be the reasons out of which his decision arises, when he acts, his responsibility for the act is uniquely his own.

> The moving finger writes, and having writ
> Moves on,
> Nor all your piety nor wit
> Can call it back to cancel half a line
> Nor all your tears wash out a word of it.

Here at last is the place where a person may discover what manner of man he is—here he may sense the independence of the self—here he may stand in his own right as a person—here Life claims him as a part of its vast creative power. It may be that in the integrity of the act a man knows for himself that he is created in the image of God, the Father of all that lives. Shrink not from your heritage by holding back when your *time* comes to *act*—for to act is to claim your true sonship.

57. To Him That Waits

"To HIM that waits, all things reveal themselves, provided that he has the courage not to deny in the darkness what he has seen in the light."

Waiting is a window opening on many landscapes. For some, waiting means the cessation of all activity when energy is gone and exhaustion is all that the heart can manage. It is the long slow panting of the spirit. There is no will to will—"spent" is the word. There is no hope, not hopelessness—there is no sense of anticipation or even awareness of a loss of hope. Perhaps even the memory of function itself has faded. There is now and before—there is no after.

For some, waiting is a time of intense preparation for the next leg of the journey. Here at last comes a moment when forces can be realigned and a new attack upon an old problem can be set in order. Or it may be a time of reassessment of all plans and of checking past failures against present insight. It may be the moment of the long look ahead when the landscape stretches far in many directions and the chance to select one's way among many choices cannot be denied.

For some, waiting is a sense of disaster of the soul. It is what Francis Thompson suggests in the line: "Naked I wait Thy love's uplifted stroke!" The last hiding place has been abandoned because even the idea of escape is without meaning. Here is no fear, no panic, only the sheer excruciation of utter disaster. It is a kind of emotional blackout in the final moment before the crash—it is the passage through the Zone of Treacherous Quiet.

For many, waiting is something more than all of this. It is the experience of recovering balance when catapulted from one's place. It is the quiet forming of a pattern of recollection in which there is called into focus the fragmentary values from myriad encounters of many kinds in a lifetime of living. It is to watch a gathering darkness until all light is swallowed up completely without the power to interfere or bring a halt. Then to continue one's journey in the darkness with one's footsteps guided by the illumination of remembered radiance is to know courage of a peculiar kind—the courage to demand that light continue to be light even in the surrounding darkness. To walk in the light while darkness invades, envelops, and surrounds is to wait on the Lord. This is to know the renewal of strength. This is to walk and faint not.

58. Making a Good Life

THERE is much conversation about making a good life. Deep within the human spirit is a concern that insists upon perfection. The distinction must be made between perfection in a particular activity, in a particular skill, and the central concern of the human spirit for perfection as a total experience. The former can be measured in terms of standards and concrete goals. I know a man who is most meticulous about many things that have their place but are inconsequential. He is so insistent about the temperature of his coffee that he neglects simple courtesy to the person who serves it.

Sometimes the attitude is more comprehensive. It has to do with staking out an area and covering it in a certain way with a satisfactory structure. It has to do with plans and their fulfillment—ends and the means by which the ends are secured. This kind of perfection often makes for arrogance of spirit and unbearable snobbery. It says to all and sundry: There is but one way to do a thing and this is that way. It does not always follow that arrogance is the result; there may be a simple pride in the beauty and the wholeness of the flawless. To behold a lovely thing in all its parts, be it a deed, a well-rounded idea, a clear, beautiful, and perfect phrase or a way of performing, is to experience a moment of glory and sheer delight.

But the central concern for perfection lies outside of all manifestations and all deeds. It is more than, and other than, all expressions of every kind, and yet it informs the ultimate character of all expressions of every kind. It is the image which the sculptor sees in the block of marble; the dream in the soul of the prophet and the seer; the profound sense of life in the spirit of the dying; the picture of the beloved in the eyes of the lover; the hope that continues when all rational grounds for confidence have been destroyed. It is what remains when all doors have finally closed and all the lights have gone out, one by one. Here at last we are face to face with what man is in his literal substance: the essence of his nobility and dignity. In religion it is called the image of the Creator and is the authentic "for instance" of the givenness of God. To be aware of this is the source of all man's confidential endurance through the vicissitudes of his living. This is to sit in judgment on every deed, however good and perfect it may be within itself—to move with reverence through all of life, always seeking and finding, always building and rebuilding, always repenting, always rejoicing. This is to walk with God.

59. Friends Whom I Knew Not

Thou hast made known to me friends whom I knew not
Thou has brought the distant near and made a brother of the stranger.

THE strength of the personal life is often found in the depth and intensity of its isolation. The fight for selfhood is unending. There is the ever-present need to stand alone, unsupported and unchallenged. To be sure of one's self, to be counted for one's self *as* one's self, is to experience aliveness in its most exciting dimension. If there is a job of work to be done that is impossible, if there is a need to be met that is limitless, if there is a word to be said that can never be said, the spirit of the whole man is mustered and in the exhaustive effort he finds *himself* in the solitariness of strength renewed and courage regained. Below the surface of all the activity and functioning in which life engages us, there is a level of disengagement when the individual is a private actor on a lonely stage. It is here that things are seen without their outer garbs—the seedlings of desires take quiet root, the bitter waters and the sweet springs find their beginnings, the tiny stirrings that become the raging tempests are seen to shimmer in the semi-darkness—this is "the region," "the place," "the clime" where man is the lonely solitary guest in the vast empty house of the world.

But this is not all of a man's life, this is not the full and solid picture. The strands of life cannot be so divided that each can be traced to a separate source. There is no mine, there is no thine. When there is that which I would claim as my very own, a second look, a subtle strangeness, something, announces that there can never be anything that is my very own. Always moving in upon a man's life is the friend whose existence he did not know, whose coming and going is not his to determine. The journeyings take many forms—sometimes it is in the vista that opens before his mind because of lines written long before in an age he did not know; sometimes it is in a simple encounter along the way when before his eyes the unknown stranger becomes the sharer of tidings that could be borne only by a friend. Sometimes a deep racial memory throws into focus an ancient wisdom that steadies the hand and stabilizes the heart. Always moving in upon a man's life is the friend whose existence he did not know, whose coming and going is not his to determine. At last, a man's life is his very own *and* a man's life is never his, alone.

60. The Temptation to Postpone

THE temptation to postpone living until some future time is very subtle—that is, to postpone living significantly. Such a temptation is apt to present itself at any time and to any person. There is the person who says, "When my ship comes in . . ." or "When my luck changes . . ." or "When I get a certain job, then I'll come into my own and begin to live." When we are very young we are apt to think that all our youth is but preliminary to the real business of living. Of course this is true but not altogether. In terms of vocational preparation or in terms of certain broad social responsibilities that are the inevitable accompaniment to adulthood, such is the case. Sometimes because of a sudden or radical reversal in circumstances, an individual may suspend all meaningful living, devoting his time and energy completely to the rugged business of recouping his position or fashioning an immediate technique of survival. Everything has to wait until the situation is in hand and normalcy is restored. Sometimes everything is held up because of a decision which someone else must make, and for a short or long interval life hangs in the balance. At such a time no plans can be made, no decisions determined; waiting, waiting, waiting—this seems to be all that can be managed.

Nevertheless, to postpone living significantly in the present is a serious blunder. Life does not stop being life because we are experiencing reverses or because we are young or because we are preparing ourselves vocationally or because certain important decisions that are in the hands of others have not been made. All of this is to give a purely quantitative character to life, to measure it exclusively in terms of the episode, the event, the circumstance. It is important to cultivate a "feeling for significance" in living and thus to give the quality of aliveness to the experience of living moment by moment. This means seeking ever for fullness, keenness, and zest as the open sesame to experienced life in the living of life. What is lived deeply is securely one's own and nothing can ever take it away—neither circumstance, nor age, nor even Death itself.

> The life that I have lived,
>   so full, so keen,
> Is mine! I hold it firm
>   beneath thy [Death] blow
> And, dying, take it with me
>   where I go.*

61. The Narrow Ridge

FOR some men there can be no security in life apart from being surrounded by the broad expanse of a country in which all landmarks are clear and the journey is along a well-worn path. Day after day they must be able to look up at any moment and know exactly where

* "Life I Lived" by Ernest Raymond, in *The New York Times Magazine*, September 27, 1959.

they are. Their lives feed on the familiar tidbits concerning those to whom one long adjustment has been made, and the possibility of the sudden shift in temperament or behavior almost never occurs. There is a strange comfort in the assurance of the commonplace and familiar. Everything is in its place and all things are arranged in a neat pattern of stability. The one great fear is the fear of change, the one great dread is the dread of strangeness.

Of course there is strength in this kind of security. Living can become routinized and reduced to the dignity of the behavior pattern. Thus the shock of the sudden encounter has a constant absorption. It is as if one's life were lived behind a sure and continuous windbreak. Days come and go and each one is as the one before. At length the monotony folds its wings and stirs no more. There is not even the pith of endurance, only the settling in and the dimming of all lights.

Buber says that life for him is at its very best when he is living on what he calls "the narrow ridge." It is a way of life that generates zest for each day's round because it is lived with anticipation. There is the full recognition of the necessity for routines and even the inner provisions for the simple monotony which is a part of all human experience. The commonplace remains the commonplace and the ordinary remains the ordinary—but this does not exhaust the meaning of the days. Each day's length is rimmed round with a margin of the joy of the unexpected, the anticipation of the new and the significant. It is to give to living a whiff of ammonia. The accent, the bias, of such a life is on the side of the margin, the overtone, rather than a mere acceptance of the commonplace and the ordinary. If such is one's prevailing attitude, then even the commonplace becomes infused with the kind of vitality that gives it a new meaning. This is not merely a matter of temperament or special gift. Such a possibility lies within reach of every man. It stems out of a conviction about the meaning of life as a whole, a faith that affirms that Life can be trusted to fulfill itself in the big Moment *and* the ordinary event, that what a man demands of life must never be more than what he is willing to believe about life. In each of us there is a "Cascade Eagle," a bird that is higher when soaring in the gorge than the highest soarer above the plains—because the gorge is in the mountains. To give this eagle wings is the call to every man.

The Quest for Love

Now abideth faith, hope, love, these three
But the greatest of these is love.

62. Tongues of Men and of Angels

"If i could speak with the tongues of men and of angels. . . ."

From the welter of sounds
Everywhere in Nature's world,
Some froze in their place
'Til clarity became their grace;
Thoughts, hopes, ideas, dreams—
These they became.
"I love you"—here all essence overflows
Or else it stalks life with empty sounds.
"Follow me"—when the Master speaks
A trumpet inflames the will
Or turns the mind away to other things.
  Words can move like balls of fire
    Where light has never been.
  Words can creep like heavy dew upon the grass.
  Words can inhabit only the twilight
    And the dawn.
  There are midnight words.
Words—Words—the seal on man's brow;
The symbol of his place among all living things.

Words need not be spoken in fullness. Words are sometimes so charged with feeling, so crowded with concentrated thought, that they are shattered, smashed, and all their churning contents spill to burn their way like liquid fire through the mind. To separate words from true and hallowed meanings, to strip them of their acquired clothes, to make them serve in strange lands in far-off places, to use them as agents of deceit, as thongs to flail and abuse, as measures of pride and illusion—all this is to degrade a most precious gift from God.

Our Father, may our words never turn on us to torment our days and crowd our nights with terror and alarm, but be ever present to bless our years because what we mean we say, and what we say we do.

63. All Mysteries and All Knowledge

"THOUGH I have the gift of prophecy, and understand all mysteries, and all knowledge. . . ."

Through slimy oozes of primeval ocean beds,
Man's body, a living thing,
Climbed slowly up the years.
By fitful steps it made its way:
    Swimming, crawling, climbing,
    No stage was skipped.
At last, held taut twixt earth and sky,
It stood upright to shout defiance to the hills.
So closed one hoary chapter;
So closed one act on a strident key.
The body was mature,
All vital organs seemed as one creative harmony
Without consent of mind.
The mind was there; mind it was not:
Taxed to the limit of its power
It kept the body safe, alive from every harm.
With life more friendly, mind released,
Thus man a living spirit, woke.

His body found the secret long ago.
But the mind can't come to rest.
Through all the aisles the fight goes on:
Impulses, instincts, fears released, hold sway.
Man wants to love; he hates.
He hurts what he would heal.
He kills what he needs preserved.
He brings blight, dread, and death.

High above the turmoil, the Voice is clear:
"Thou art made for wholeness,
Body, mind, spirit: one creative synthesis,
Moving in perfect harmony within, without,
With fellow man and nature all around
To make Heaven where Hell is found."

64. It Profiteth Me Nothing

"THOUGH I give my body to be burned . . . it profiteth me nothing. . . ."

A man may live out all his days
Tensing every nerve to do his best
To find at last a dead goal, a false road.
How may he know?
Is there no guide for man?
No shining light by which his steps are led?
Through all the chaos of his years
He seeks to know.
　Some say, "Do this, do that,"
　Or "Give up your goods. Hold nothing back
　And free yourself to find *your* way."
　Again "Commit your way to something good
　That makes upon your life the great demand.
　Place upon the altar all hopes and dreams
　Leaving no thing untouched, no thing unclaimed."
And yet, no peace . . .
　"What more?" I ask with troubled mind.
　The answer . . . moving stillness.
And then
　The burning stare of the eyes of God
　Pierces my inmost core
　Beyond my strength, beyond my weakness,
　Beyond what I am,

Beyond what I would be
Until my refuge is in Him alone.

"This . . . This above all else I claim," God says.

65. Love Is Kind

"LOVE suffereth long, and is kind. . . ."

"You are so kind!"
Familiar words, a harvest of gratitude
Planted by years of life.
Simple fruit of simple deeds
Where no duty bound
And the heart was free.
There is praise for the brave act
When odds are weighed, decisions made
For action clear and unrestrained.
There is honor for mercies shared
With all who need without demand
The careless grace that heals, redeems.
There is reverence for all:
The good, the bad, the weak, the strong
Whose only claim is the Light within,
The gift of God to all mankind.

But for kindness, what?
Search everywhere—the earth, the sea
And all the reaches of the stars,
There is no home where dwells with merit sure
The man whose claim to grace is held secure!
Grace knows no bars.
There is no loss that binds;
Requitement, duty, balanced deeds
Are strangers here.

The heart pours forth what it cannot hold,
A living spirit of purest love.

66. Thinketh No Evil

"LOVE . . . is not puffed up . . . thinketh no evil. . . "

The murky motive is the common lot!
Its dwelling place the human heart.
To find its source, to clean it out,
A lifetime's quest is far too short.
But claims of victory abound:
Ancient Adam makes a fateful choice
And all his sons are doomed to pay.
The will diseased at time of birth
And sin holds sway without restraint.
In vain man seeks the starting place.
The search goes on to find a clue
Somewhere along the way that he must take:
If all else were quiet,
And in the waiting stillness
I could hear the clear command
That marshaled all my life to a single stand,
Then would I see to move in step
With motive clean!

How can this be?
    So much of me is held by you;
    So much remains in other days
    Long since forgotten or remembered ill;
    So much was left along the way
    And only stain to mark its place.
    Oh, what a scattering there is!
    What can deliver from this living death?
    Only love—that God can give.

67. Rejoiceth Not in Iniquity

"REJOICETH not in iniquity, but rejoiceth in the truth. . . ."

Nestled underneath a sheaf of old papers
Carefully protected from hungry cats
I found five moist-eyed mice.
A surging impulse of destruction filled my mind.
The thirst of a thousand aeons of the *will to kill*
Stilled any newborn dream that life is one.
And yet, I paused!
Reflection held me bound:
Who am I that I should crush in a single blow
The throbbing pulse of life caught in these tiny forms?
Are they not life?
To let them live would be to run the risk of death
From pestilence, disease, or plague.
How to destroy and yet not feel
That some of me had died?
No sudden dying this:
   A slow falling away of grace,
   A little hardening of the heart,
   A bit less sensitive to wrong,
   A look away from mercy's claim.
Can a mouse enjoy life?
Is there a secret that he holds I dare not miss?
But the choice of life or death was mine to make.
To the nestling mice I was Almighty.
Can Omnipotence know aught but power?
What are its bounds, its laws?
What holds it in its place?
Perched on the pinnacle of that dreadful moment
I saw the heights, the depths, of all brutality.
The bloody clue to the crimson stain in man's uneasy past
   flashed before me.

To power, stark without restraint in time or circumstance,
What are ethics, morals, mercy's claim?
Weakness, betrayal, sentiment?
It was all clear!
To grant man power and hazard the trust
That he would find a way to make life safe;
Secure for all that lives!
This was God's great hope
When into man He blew the breath of life!

68. Endureth All Things

"LOVE . . . hopeth all things, endureth all things. . . ."

The contradictions of experience confuse, confound!
Tides of beauty caught in an undertow of slime;
Goodness, luminous, refined,
Manacled by evil no hand can stay;
Love, ripe and full,
Stalked by hate that binds and chokes;
Hope, leaping clear from peak to peak,
Haunted by echoes of despair!
The contradictions of experience confuse, confound!
Which is the true, the sure, the real?
The final vote of man's spirit,
What does it say?
Is there Eternal Drama here
Endless in interval, whole in itself?
Is the tension only shadow,
A trick of mind, a whimper in the heart
And nothing more?
The closing vote—what does it say?
The contradictions are final?
Never!
The growing edge of hope remains
When all the voices of despair are stilled.

Love persists when hate no longer holds.
Goodness triumphs though evil struggles to the end.
All this man's spirit says.
The dogmas of the mind are afterthoughts;
So let the winds blow!
Let the torrents fume!
Let the night wax in darkness!
Let death be death—
Life will not die!
Life holds and grows.

69. Knowledge . . . Shall Vanish Away

"WHETHER there be knowledge, it shall vanish away. . . ."

A ceaseless search like the ebb and flow of oceans
Marks all man's days:
For him no rest, no rest;
The fever in the blood
Is answer to the temper of the mind.

When Time was young, just learning how to walk,
It placed its stamp on the single cell
Which gave a slant to all that lives
Today or yesterday, no matter when.
A ceaseless search like the ebb and flow of oceans
Marks all man's days.

Is there some point, some place of rest
To bring an end to all man's quest?
Something that does not fail?
Something that lasts beyond all things that pass
When shadows thicken and the lights grow dim?
Some worldly hope that gives retreat
From all the winds that beat upon the world?
Some sure attachment to another's life

That stands secure against all change of mind or heart?
Some private dream where only dwells
The purest secrets of desire?
All these must fade,
All these must pass away.

There is a sense of wholeness at the core of man
That must abound in all he does;
That marks with reverence his ev'ry step;
That has its sway when all else fails;
That wearies out all evil things;
That warms the depth of frozen fears
Making friend of foe,
Making love of hate,
And lasts beyond the living and the dead,
Beyond the goals of peace, the ends of war!
This man seeks through all his years:
To be complete and of one piece, within, without.

70. For We Know in Part

"FOR we know in part, and we prophecy in part. . . ."

The sense of self is fully known
When a man can say, "I did it."
Such triumph who can claim?
In every deed are many streams
Whose sources lie beyond all dreams,
Or sleep within the womb of ancient myths.

The words in his tongue, wanderers all,
Finding in man a short-spanned place—
They're never his alone.
O'er what a way they've come!
Through countless years in every land,
Through crucibles of every mood

Words now familiar in their place
Have made their own the marks of many minds.
How dare a man say, "I—I speak"?

Free-flowing thoughts from living minds
Are big with residues of other times
Forced from their place by inner law,
Compelled to rest in little spells;
A man may never say, "This thought is mine."
An equity in thoughts is his;
The rest belongs to every man.

Fierce, private, intimate, unique
Feelings spring from deep within;
A boundless inner world as old as life—
They come, without command.
The feeling tone, the pointed shape
Carries the image of the man.
To this he gives his own life's plan,
No more than this is his to claim.

All knowledge in whatever form
Maintains its place, secure.
It knows no lord, no single mind.
Its harvest ripens as it will.
Its secret is its own to give,
In part, to share with other minds.
To say "I know" is always false,
However sure the words may seem.
Before the echo fades, the lights go out,
The man is held by fear, by doubt.
To seek, to find, to seek again,
This is man's journey, this his way.

71. Comes That Which Is Perfect

"BUT when that which is perfect is come, that which is in part shall be done away."

Of all the stories Jesus told,
There is none more deadly where it strikes
Than what he said about the man
Who came to feast with wedding guests
Without the proper dress.
One precious moment all his own, to bring to life
His only gift.
Nameless, unclaimed, the moments come and go,
The smooth unfolding of each passing day
Weans the life from earlier dreams,
Dulls the sharp edges of the mind.
Days are but days, and nights but interludes
Before the sound begins again.
And then one moment, unlike all the rest,
Descends upon his world.
It comes unheralded, but it bears his name!
The one desire which all his years have sought
Stands ripe for plucking before his startled eyes;
The one great vision from the heights
That launched him on his way when life was young;
The perfect love to make his life complete . . .
But always the fatal flaw.
The refrain's the same;
The wedding feast is on;
Down the long banquet hall, the King appears.
He sees the careless dress, the half-brushed hair,
In the wary eyes the slow chagrin.
Excuses, fears, or alibis can find no voice.
An aweful stillness freezes everything.
The Moment burns itself away

Then passes even as it came.
And what is left? Stark despair
Where nothing lives;
The Dream has died.

72. When I was a Child

"WHEN I was a child, I spake as a child. . . ."

"This man is innocent."
The words are heard on many tongues.
Where deeds can find no resting place,
They lift the load that guilt would yield;
Hidden behind their empty shield
The wounds the years can't heal remain.
A name is ruined, the delicate fabric is ripped,
Is torn.
Innocence may be more than this:
    Something that has never been tested, never tried.
    No ordeal has scorched its brow;
    Pure of conscious wrong, or felt mistake,
    There is no wisdom it has learned to know.
    Such is the beauty of the rose.
But the beauty of the oak is something more.

The child is innocent!
A man is not; he is never pure.
He has chronicled too many days,
Tasted in fact or mind forbidden fruit,
Been caught and held by many drives,
Immune to ends of virtue in a single mind,
To be innocent, to be pure.
    If he has kneaded ugliness until beauty stands revealed;
    If he has wrestled with the open independence of the sea,
    Until he holds the secrets of storm and calm;
    If he has walked through flames, felt their searing,

Until the dross of all mistakes has been consumed;
If he has fought with inward foes
Until every weakness of his life has shown its face—
This is to triumph, this is to know.

This is to be the good he seeks.
This is to know the God he knew.

73. But Then Face to Face

"FOR now we see through a glass, darkly; but then face to face. . . ."

It is the judgment scene.
The climax of man's life has come at last;
The oriental despot sits enthroned.
Before him come the peoples of the earth.
Here are no men, no women, boys or girls
Struggling for rank, wealth, class, or power.
No race or tribe has standing here.
All walls that separate, divide,
By the moving drama are pushed aside.
Each life is freed of all pretense,
Each shadowy seeming swept away
By the mighty spread of ceaseless light.
   "I was sick, comfortless;
   I was hungry and desperate;
   I was lonely, wretched;
   I was in prison, forsaken . . ."
Strange awful words from Him;
Words more searching followed after:
   "I know your tasks were manifold;
   Unyielding claims consumed your thoughts.
   There was no time to be at ease with deeds,
   To give yourself beyond your creed.
   Oh, I know about your temperament, your health,
   Somehow you could not manage all your chores,

Excuses came to reinforce the empty feeling of your heart.
I know how hard it was for you.
You did not want to be an easy touch!
Beyond all else, your ties of blood;
Charity must begin at home.
Besides,
    You did not know, but are you sure?
    Do you recall the flashes of concern
    That held you in your place that day?
    I see you do remember well.
    Again they came and then again,
    Until at last they came no more;
    Only the hollow darkness of the self cut off
    From all the pain and pathos of the world.
    No word of mine can alter what your days have done."
The story of your life is what the judge reveals.
From the relentless judgment, is there no appeal?

74. The Greatest of These

"Now abideth faith, hope, love, these three; but the greatest of these
is love."

> "While there is a lower class
>   I am in it.
> While there is a criminal element
>   I am of it.
> While there is a man in jail
>   I am not free."

Thus spoke a man whose life, whose deeds
These words fulfilled.
Contacts across all barriers abound
Where the world is narrowed in fact and dream.
If there is found no will to love
To make an act of grace toward fellow men,

Contacts degrade, outrage, destroy
The tender shoots of simple trust.
Love abides where all else dies
From sheer revulsion and disgust.
The fruit it bears sustains the nerve,
Strengthens the weak, the insecure,
Breaks the chains of fear that
Hold the minds of men in hate's embrace,
Condemns the things that shrink the soul.
It is the "precious bane" for those who seek
To know the Way of God among the sons of men.
It meets men where they are, cruel,
Lustful, greedy, callous, of low design—
It treats them there, as if they were full grown
And crowned with all that God would have them be.
For love's own sake and that alone,
Men do with joyous hope and quiet calm
What no command of Life or Death could force of them
If love were not.
To be God's child, to love with steady mind,
With fervent heart, this is to know
The Truth that makes man free.

The Quest for Peace

Lord, make me an Instrument of Thy Peace.

75. Make Me an Instrument of Thy Peace

"LORD, make me an instrument of Thy Peace." These words, taken from the prayer of St. Francis, speak to one of the most insistent conditions of the human spirit. It is not easy to be an instrument of peace because we understand so little about the anatomy of hostility and its particular kind of etiquette. Again and again we use our words to protect ourselves, to "put others in their place," to humiliate and to wound; sometimes, quite unconsciously. Have you ever been caught in the backwash of your words which hit their mark, resulting in an injury which was not a part of your intent? All of this because you were too preoccupied with your own interests, your own concerns to take into account the other person? At such a moment your good word may easily become an instrument of violence.

Ask yourself, "Have I ever indulged in gossip which gave me an opportunity to say something uncharitable about someone else? Of course, if I had not heard the gossip and passed it on, then there would have been no chance for me to express my quiet hostility and, at the same time, be relieved of the responsibility for it. When I participate in the shared rumors and the gossip around me by passing them on or by refraining from stopping them with what I know to be the facts and the truth, I let my attitude and my influence become instruments of violence in my hands."

I offer my prayer to God:

"Lord, make me an instrument of Thy Peace." Teach me how to order my days that with sure touch I may say the right word at the right time and in the right way—lest I betray the spirit of peace. Let me not be deceived by my own insecurity and weakness which would make me hurt another as I try desperately to help myself.

Keep watch with me, O my Father, over the days of my life, that with abiding enthusiasm I may be in such possession of myself that each day I may offer to Thee the full, unhampered use of me in all my parts as "an instrument of Thy Peace." Amen.

76. Contradictions Not Final

TWO MEN faced each other in a prison cell. They belonged to different countries, their roots watered by streams from different cultures. One was under sentence of death, scheduled to be executed within a few short hours. The other was a visitor and friend—this, even though months before they had been enemies in a great war. They bade each other farewell for the last time. The visitor was deeply troubled, but he could not find his way through the emotional maze in which he was caught to give voice to what cried out for utterance. This is what he wanted to say but could not:

"We may not be able to stop and undo the hard old wrongs of the great world outside, but through you and me no evil shall come either in the unknown where you are going, or in this imperfect and haunted dimension of awareness through which I move. Thus between us we shall cancel out all private and personal evil, thus arrest private and personal consequences to blind action and reaction, thus prevent specifically the general incomprehension and misunderstanding, hatred and revenge of our time from spreading further!"

The forces at work in the world which seem to determine the future and the fate of mankind seem so vast, impersonal, and unresponsive to the will and desire of any individual that it is easy to abandon all hope for a sane and peaceful order of life for mankind. Nevertheless, it is urgent to hold steadily in mind the utter responsibility of the solitary individual to do everything with all his heart and mind to arrest the development of the consequence of private and personal evil resulting from the interaction of the impersonal forces that surround us. To cancel out between you and another all personal and private evil, to put your life squarely on the side of the good thing because it is good, and for no other reason, is to anticipate the Kingdom of God at the level of your functioning.

At long last a man must be deeply convinced that the contradictions of life which he encounters are not final, that the radical tension between good and evil, as he sees it and feels it, does not have the last word about the meaning of life and the nature of existence, that there is a spirit in man and in the world working always against the thing that destroys and cuts down. Thus he will live wisely and courageously his little life, and those who see the sunlight in his face will drop their tools and follow him. There is no ultimate negation for the man for whom it is categorical that the ultimate destiny of man on this planet is a good destiny.

77. A Prayer for Peace

OUR FATHER, fresh from the world with the smell of life upon us, we make an act of prayer in the silence of this place. Our minds are troubled because the anxieties of our hearts are deep and searching. We are stifled by the odor of death which envelopes the earth because in so many places brother fights against brother. The panic of fear, the torture of insecurity, the ache of hunger—all have fed and rekindled ancient hatreds and long-forgotten memories of old struggles when the world was young and Thy children were but dimly aware of Thy Presence in the midst. For all this we seek forgiveness. There is no one of us without guilt, and before Thee we confess our sins: we are proud and arrogant; we are selfish and greedy; we have harbored in our hearts and minds much that makes for bitterness, hatred, and revenge.

While we wait in Thy Presence, search our spirits and grant to our minds the guidance and the wisdom that will teach us the way to take, without which there can be no peace and no confidence anywhere. Teach us how to put at the disposal of Thy Purposes of Peace the fruits of our industry, the products of our minds, the vast wealth of our land, and the resources of our spirit. Grant unto us the courage to follow the illumination of this hour to the end that we shall not lead death to any man's door, but rather may we strengthen the hands of all in high places and in common tasks who seek to build a friendly world of friendly men, beneath a friendly sky. This is the simple desire of our hearts which we share with Thee in quiet confidence. Amen.

78. Remain at Peace

"ACCUSTOM yourself to remain at peace in the depth of your heart, in spite of your restless imagination."

Peace anywhere seems to be wishful thinking during the days of turmoils within and violences without. Peace of mind, peace of heart, peace of home, peace of country, peace of world, peace of cosmos— it does not matter which, the same sense of pinpoint unreality pervades. There seems to be a vast stirring of energy, malignant and unstructured, that catapults to the surface all kinds of disharmonies, conflicts, and disorders. The Middle East, the Far East, South Africa, North Africa, West Africa, Hungary, Poland, France, Germany, Russia, the Indian Nations of the Americas, the continental United States viewed by section, state, or city—always there is present the turbulent quality, the out-of-hand aspect, of the common life.

Years ago a free-lance writer visited Dr. M. W. Locke, the famous Canadian physician. The technique he used in treatment of bodily ills had to do with foot manipulation. A little crippled girl sat in the chair before the doctor. Very gently he began massaging her crippled limb—then he gave the foot a sudden manipulation. The girl screamed! A shudder went through the people waiting their turn. In the afternoon, the writer saw the father of the little girl and offered sympathy.

"Thank you very much," said the father. "But you do not understand. When my daughter first came here several weeks ago, the doctor could do anything to her foot and she could not feel it. When I heard her cry aloud this morning I said, 'Thank God, life is in her foot at last.' "

The stirring of energy in myriad forms of unstructured malevolences may well be the spirit of Life, of God at work in behalf of new life and perhaps a new creation on this planet. We must find our place in the areas of the new vitalities, the place where the old is breaking up and the new is being born. What a moment to be alive and, more importantly, to be aware! Of course, this we cannot do unless we are able to gather unto ourselves the wise caution of Fénelon, "Accustom yourself to remain at peace in the depth of your heart, in spite of your restless imagination." God grant this for each of us.

79. To Die or Not to Die

THE HOUR was long past midnight. Our talk had begun in the early evening. It seemed that the first few hours had been spent in a preliminary exploring of each other's mind, spirit, and reactions to life and its undertones. At last he turned to me with a full, distant stare in his eyes—eyes that looked beyond me, the room, the city— beyond all things present. I felt as if I were in the presence of something unlawful to be exposed. I waited. The sounds of the night, first distant and then close at hand, came from the outer darkness and the city street: the steady churning rhythm of the cable of the cable car, a passing automobile, the bark of my neighbor's dog, the mating howl of the cats on the back fence, and far away as if from some outer planet, the periodic moan of the fog horn. At length I was aware that he had begun to speak. My mind finally focused on the sound of his voice:

"True it is that there are some things in life that are worse than death. This I have thought for a long time but tonight I am not so sure. For the assumption is that death is always a live option—a choice that a man can make rather than to do a thing that defames his soul so that life, under the condition, is a strain and a desecration...." There was a long pause as he held his right hand before his eyes as if he were seeing it for the first time. After an age of silence he spoke again:

"But suppose you cannot die. Do you know what I mean? A thousand years ago in another land it seems I was a political prisoner. With firmness of spirit and will I made my choice. 'I will let them kill me. I will choose death rather than betray my soul.' Not once, but many times, I was brought to the very brink of death—twice, I remember, I was just a hairbreadth from the beyond and with all

108

the power of my being I tried to push myself over to the other side. But with the cunningness of inspired demons, death was robbed . . . Until at last my will, my spirit, my whole self was splintered but I could not die. There was nothing left within me to rally; I was exhausted—not merely my body, my nerves, my emotions—No! But I was exhausted, spent, wasted. Everything sacred to me was betrayed. The war ended. I was released. I ask you—do you think I can ever be a man again?"

80. Let Us Remember the Children

THERE is a strange power inherent in the spirit of man. Sitting or standing or lying in one place, he can bring before his presence those long separated from him by distance or by death, those whose plight he understands but whose faces he has never seen and whose names register in him no meaning.

Let us bring before our spirits the children of the world! The children born in refugee camps where all is tentative and shadowy, except the hardness of the constant anguish and anxiety that have settled deep within the eyes of those who answer when the call is "Mommy" or "Daddy" . . . the numberless host of orphans corralled like sheep in places of refuge where the common conscience provides bread to eat, water to drink, and clothes to cover the nakedness and the shame . . . the inarticulate groan of those who are the offspring of hot lust held in its place by exploding shells and the insanity of war—these are the special wards of the collective guilt of the human race, the brood left behind when armies moved and the strategy of war made towns into a desolation. The illegitimate children of peacetime, who have no peg upon which to hang the identity of meaning, whose tender lives are cut adrift from all harbors of refuge and security—these are choked by a shame not of their making and who look upon their own existence with heartache and humiliation. The children in families where all love is perishing and they cannot even sense the awareness that their own lives are touched by love's gentleness and strength. The sick children who were ushered into the world as if their bodies were maimed and twisted by disaster which was their lot in some encounter before the fullness of time gave them birth among the children of men. Those who played and romped on the hillside but now will never walk again. Those who once enjoyed the beauty of sky and earth, who looked upon everything about them with unsullied wonder, but who are closed in darkness never to see again. The children of the halting, stumbling mind in whom some precious ingredient is lacking, leaving in its place the vacant mindless stare. The children of great and good fortune whose lives have been always surrounded by the tenderness of affection and the gentleness of understanding, across whose paths no shadows have fallen and for whom life is beautiful and free—

What we bring before our presence, our Father, we share with Thee in our time of quiet and prayer. We thank Thee for the gift to do this, the strange power inherent in our spirits. Grant that what we see in this way may not leave us untouched but may inspire us to be active, responsive instruments in Thy hands to heal Thy children, to bless Thy children, to redeem Thy children. Amen.

81. The Idol of Togetherness

"IF THY soul is a stranger to thee, the whole world is unhomely."

The fight for the private life is fierce and unyielding. Often it seems as if our times are in league with the enemy. There is little rhythm of alternation between the individual and the others. Land values are so high that breathing space around the places where we live is cut away. We flee from the crowded city to the quiet of the countryside. But the countryside becomes jammed with the sounds, the noises, the sights, the pressures which were left behind. Sometimes we escape into the city from the country.

Because of the disintegration of the mood of tenderness that has overtaken us we falter in our understanding of one another. There is a certain kind of understanding abroad—it is understanding that invades, snoops, threatens, and makes afraid or embarrasses. The craftsmen of the public taste move in upon us, seeking to determine the kind of food we eat, the soap we use, the make of car we drive, and the best way to brush our teeth. What has become of the person, the private wish?

We have made an idol of togetherness. It is the watchword of our times, it is more and more the substitute for God. In the great huddle we are desolate, lonely, and afraid. Our shoulders touch but our hearts cry out for understanding without which there can be no life and no meaning. The Great Cause, even the Cause of Survival, is not enough! There must be found ever-creative ways that can ventilate the private soul without blowing it away, that can confirm and affirm the integrity of the person in the midst of the collective necessities of our times.

There is within reach of every man a defense against the Grand Invasion. He can seek deliberately to become intimately acquainted with himself. He can cultivate an enriching life with persons, enhancing the private meaning and the personal worth. He can grow in the experience of solitude, companioned by the minds and spirits who, as Pilgrims of the Lonely Road, have left logs of their journey. He can become at home, within, by locating in his own spirit the trysting place where he and his God may meet; for it is here that life becomes *private* without being *self-centered,* that the little purposes that cloy may be absorbed in the Big Purpose that structures and redefines, that the individual comes to himself, the wanderer is home, and the private life is saved for deliberate involvement.

82. The Need for Periodic Rest

THE NEED for periodic rest is not confined to mechanisms of various kinds. Rest may be complete inactivity when all customary functioning is suspended and everything comes to a pause. Rest may be a variation in intensity, a contrast between loud and soft, high and low, strong and weak, a change of pace. Rest may be a complete shifting of scenery by the movement of objects or the person. All things seem to be held in place by the stability of a rhythm that holds and releases but never lets go.

Under this same necessity lives the mind as well. There is an inner characteristic of mind that shares profoundly in the rhythm that holds and releases but never lets go. Rest for the mind takes many forms: it may come in the change of material upon which it works; it may be ranging widely and irresponsibly over strange areas of thought; it may be tackling a tough problem with more than the customary intensity; it may be daydreaming, that strange and wonderful fairyland of sugar plums and candies; it may be the experience of being swept to a perilous height by a sudden gale that rushes in from some distant shore or of being caught in the churning spiral of a water spout that moves up from some hidden depth; it may be all, any, or none of these but something else again. Rest for the mind may be a part of its activity! Thus working and resting are a single thing. Perhaps this is true because the mind takes its energy neat, in a manner direct and immediate.

Under the same necessity lives the spirit as well. There is no clear distinction between mind and spirit; but there is a quality of mind that is more than thought and the process of thought: this quality involves feelings and the wholeness in which the life of man has its being. There is no need to tarry over the correctness of definition or even over the preciseness of meaning. What is being considered is what a man means totally when he says, "I am." This "self" shares profoundly in the rhythm that holds and releases but never lets go. There is the rest of detachment and withdrawal when the spirit moves into the depths of the region of the Great Silence, where world weariness is washed away and blurred vision is once again prepared for the focus of the long view where seeking and finding are so united that failure and frustration, real though they are, are no longer felt to be ultimately real. Here the Presence of God is sensed as an all-pervasive aliveness which materializes into the concreteness of communion: the reality of prayer. Here God speaks without words and the self listens without ears. Here at last, glimpses of the meaning of all things and the meaning of one's own life are seen with all their strivings. To accept this is one meaning of the good line, "Rest in the Lord—O, rest in the Lord."

83. Twilights and Endless Landscapes

THE intimate and gentle blanket of twilight had covered the desert with a softness highlighted by the restrained radiance of the disappearing sun. All the fears of war, the terrible bitterness of the market place, the deep insecurities of modern life, seemed far removed from the surrounding quiet.

Long before the coming of cities, long before the coming of men, there were twilights, radiant and glowing skies and endless landscapes. It may be that long after the earth has reclaimed the cities and the last traces of man's fevered life have been gathered into the Great Quiet, there will be twilights, radiant and glowing skies and endless landscapes.

It is not because man and his cities are not significant that they cannot outlast the twilights, the radiant and glowing skies and the endless landscapes. But their significance is of another kind. Man and his cities spring out of the earth, they are the children of the Great Womb that breathes through twilights, radiant and glowing skies and endless landscapes. Man and his cities, caught in the web their dreams inspire, manage to push the twilights out of mind. They wear themselves out and they forget from whence they come and in what at long last they find their strength. Their dreams become nightmares, their hopes become fears, and the same story repeats itself; they are claimed in the end by the twilights, the radiant and glowing skies and endless landscapes.

The more hectic the life of the cities, the more greedy and lustful the heart and mind of man, the more he forgets the meaning of the twilights, the radiant and glowing skies and endless landscapes. It is not too late. Man and his cities may yet be saved. There is still time to remember that there is twilight, the creative isthmus joining day with night. It is the time of pause when nature changes her guard. It is the lung of time by which the rhythmic respiration of day and night are guaranteed and sustained. All living things would fade and die from too much light or too much darkness, if twilight were not. In the midst of all the madness of the present hour, twilights remain and shall settle down upon the world at the close of day and usher in the nights in endless succession, despite bombs, rockets, and flying death. This is good to remember.

Even though they look down upon the ruin of cities and the fall of man, radiant and glowing skies will still trumpet their glory to the God of Life. Death and destruction cannot permanently obscure their wonder or drown their song. To remember this is to safeguard each day with the margin of strength that invades the soul from the radiant and glowing skies. These declare the glory and the tenderness of God.

84. To Make a Rest of Motion

IT IS ever a grace and a benediction to be able to come to a halt, to stop, to pause, to make a rest of motion. Thus we are privileged to turn aside from the things that occupy and preoccupy our minds in the daily round, to take a long intimate look at ourselves both in retrospect and prospect. The fever of our spirits regarded so necessary to keep us going, to make for the precise and ready functioning of our lives, can settle itself into a pervasive calm while we watch the tension drain away . . . Ah! this is very good.

It is at such times that we are free to remember! From within the quiet of our spirits we may see with startling clarity the meaning of past experiences separated in time but one in quality, sense the undercurrents of our lives and the distant shores toward which their movement points; hear the inner accent of the word spoken in haste or anger and know the quality of the hurt it gave; and feel the depths of our hunger for the wisdom that transcends all our knowledge and our understanding but is always obscured by the binding tyranny of our fact.

It is at such times that we are free to feel tomorrow as a single moment in time or as a personal event or as our exclusive and private portion; plans that are yet to unfold are seen in full dress and in utter completion; hopes that are held in chains by fears that have companioned us from our youth, are free to move and *be,* in all their glory and fulfillment; thoughts that live in hidden crevices and dark

places of the mind are seen in the radiance of complete and un-
fettered contemplation; persons from whom we are separated in space
and time can be experienced as the living present untouched by
distance or by death . . .

And beyond all this, at such times we can know the Spirit of the
living God, not as idea or form but as an enveloping Presence
energizing all the parts of our being with inspiration, enthusiasm, and
joy. It *is* ever a grace and a benediction to be able to come to a halt,
to stop, to pause, to make a rest of motion.

The Quest for God

Man without God is a seed upon the wind.

85. A Seed upon the Wind

"MAN without God is a seed upon the wind." What a picture! A tiny, living thing awaiting its moment of fulfillment, caught up in the movement of tremendous energy, is at the mercy of forces that are not responsive to its own ends! There is a grand unconscious vitality unfolding with mounting energy its impersonal purpose. In the grip of something like this, what is a tiny seed—no more than a particle of dust, a nameless nothing. Here is the abandonment of all purpose, stark helplessness without mooring or anchor. The fact that there is locked within the seed a private world of pattern and design makes no difference to the fierce velocities that sweep it on the reckless, relentless way.

"Man without God is a seed upon the wind." He is a victim of the currents of life that carry him where they will with a bland unmindfulness of purposes and ends which belong to him as a living, thinking, feeling creature. It means that such a man has no sense of center. He takes his clue to all meaning and values from the passing moment, the transitory event, the immediate issue of his day. He is at home nowhere because he is not at home "somewhere." The Master speaks of this in his direct question: "What would a man give in exchange for his soul?"

But there is a sense in which a man *with* God is a seed upon the wind—the man who has made the primary surrender, the commitment, the yielding to God at the core of his being. He is one who has relaxed his will to exercise and hold firm the initiative over his own life. This does not come without exacting struggle of the soul. One by one the outposts of his spirit are captured, retaken and lost again through hours, months, even years of warfare, until at last the very citadel of his spirit is under siege and he is subjected to an utter yielding. There follows often the long silence when nothing stirs. Then out of the quiet of his vanquished spirit something stirs and a new life emerges that belongs more to God than to self. The movement now rests with Purposes that are beyond the little purposes, with Ends that transcend the private ends, the Purposes and Ends of God. There is a sense in which a man *with* God is a seed upon the wind.

86. The Integrity of the Person

THERE is something strangely comforting and reassuring about the private pretensions under which we live. It is a matter of no little significance to know that for each of us there is a world apart in which the intimacy of thoughts and feelings may be safe from attack and violation. Much of what we mean by communication is limited to the deliberate choosing of thoughts, ideas, sentiments, feelings, which we direct toward others—yielding only the meaning that we intend, which may not be the meaning that is either true or honest. In time we develop a dependence upon the impact which we make on others as the major source from which we draw an understanding of ourselves.

I am impressed by the stories which have come to us concerning the life of the American Indian at a time far removed from the present. To him, so the accounts reveal, the Great Spirit brooded over all of life in general and particular. Before he went hunting, he invoked the Great Spirit. When crops were planted, when there was death and birth, he invoked the Great Spirit. In fine, all the common and special experiences of life were seen as being under the scrutiny and sponsorship of the Great Spirit. This meant that there was ever available the opportunity and the necessity for being genuine—the wall between the inner and the outer was very thin and transparent. *The integrity of the act* sprang out of *the integrity of the person.* There was no need to pretend. One dare not pretend to the Great Spirit.

A crushing part of the sophistication of modern life is the phenomenal rise in the feeling for a protective covering that will make the integrity of the act an awkward procedure. Why is it that we are embarrassed by simple honesty and directness in our communication with one another? And yet the hunger deepens and becomes more and more insistent for ridding ourselves of the tremendous burden of pretensions. We long for relationships in which it is no longer needful for us to pretend anything. The clue to the answer is in the awakening within us of the sense of living our lives consciously in God's presence. The habit of exposing the life, the motives, the dreams, the desires, the sins, all to God makes for *the integrity of the person*. Out of this flows *the integrity of the act*.

> Search me, O God, and know my heart,
> Try me and know my thoughts.

87. In His Image

MANY years ago a brilliant young sociologist at Columbia College delivered a lecture to his class on the "Philosophy of a Fool." He ends the first part of his address with these words: "On the seventh day, therefore, God could not rest. In the morning and the evening He busied Himself with terrible and beautiful concoctions and in the twilight of the seventh day He finished that which is of more import than the beasts of the earth and the fish of the sea and the lights of the firmament. And he called it Imagination because it was made in His own image; and those unto whom it is given shall see God."

We are accustomed to thinking of the imagination as a useful tool in the hands of the artist as he reproduces in varied forms that which he sees beyond the rim of fact that encircles him. There are times when the imagination is regarded as a delightful and often whimsical characteristic of what we are pleased to call "the childish mind." Our judgment trembles on the edge of condescension, pity, or even ridicule when imagination is confused with fancy in the reports that are given of the inner workings of the mind of the "simpleton" or "the fool." We recognize and applaud the bold and audacious leap of the mind of the scientist when it soars far out beyond that which is known and established, to fix a beachhead on distant, unexplored shores.

But the place where the imagination shows its greatest powers as the *angelos* of God is in the miracle which it creates when one man, standing in his place, is able, while remaining there, to put himself in another man's place. To send his imagination forth to establish a beachhead in another man's spirit, and from that vantage point so to blend with the other's landscape that what he sees and feels is authentic—this is the great adventure in human relations. But this is not enough. The imagination must report its findings accurately without regard to all prejudgments and private or collective fears. But this is not enough. There must be both a spontaneous and a calculating response to such knowledge which will result in sharing of resources at their deepest level.

Very glibly are we apt to use such words as "sympathy," "companion," "sitting where they sit," but to experience their meaning is to be rocked to one's foundations. The simple truth is, we resist making room for considerations that swerve us out of the path of preoccupation with ourselves, our needs, our problems. We make our imagination a thing of corruption when we give it range only over our own affairs. Here we experience the magnification of our own ills, the distortion of our own problems, and the enlargement of the areas of our misery. What we do not permit our imagination to do in the work of understanding others, turns in upon ourselves with disaster and sometimes terror.

To be to another human being what is needed at the time that the need is most urgent and most acutely felt—this is to participate in the precise act of redemption. The imagination acting under the most stringent orders can develop a technique all its own in locating and reporting to us its findings. We are not the other persons, we are ourselves. All that they are experiencing we can never know—but we can make accurate soundings which, when properly read, will enable us to be to them what we could never be without such awareness. The degree to which our imagination becomes the *angelos* of God, we ourselves may become *His instruments.*

88. The Sacrament of Remembrance

FOR US this is a moment of recollection—a sacrament of remembrance. We bring before our minds and our spirits, supported by the sureness of our feeling, those whom we love deeply, and their needs: those who are sick of body or tormented of mind; those who are now, this moment, wrestling with great and eager temptation, who fall again and again and again; those whom we love but find it, oh, so hard, to like; those whom we love but find it, oh, so hard to trust. We bring them, each one of them, before our own minds, and we tarry in and with their spirits.

We remember the little children. We call to mind those whom we have had and lost; those whom we have longed to have but never had; those whom we can never have and whose lives will never bless our own because for us the time, the season, has passed. All the children of the world: those we know well and intimately; those whose stories have crept into our minds through word of mouth or through devious ways—the hungry children, the destitute children, the starving, frightened, scarred, bedraggled children; we bring quietly and sensitively before our minds and spirits, all children.

We remember the old and the aging: those who have banked their fires long since and are waiting in the wings for the final shuffle across the stage; those who have been deserted and left in their solitariness, their loneliness, even their memories shattered. We bring before our minds and spirits the old and the aging.

Our Father, we are burdened with our recollections and we struggle beneath the weight of our memories. We seek how we may offer all to Thee in the quietness of our own inward parts, in the silence of this place. Brood over ourselves and our recollections with Thy spirit until at last there may grow up within us insight, wisdom, and new levels of sensitiveness that we may be redemptive in all that we do this day and beyond. Our need, O God, is great! Amen.

89. We Spend Our Lives Before Thee

THE STORY of our lives is the old story of man. There is the insistent need to separate ourselves from the tasks by which our days are surrounded. The urgency within us cries out for detachment from the traffic and the complexities of our involvements. There is the ebb and flow of anxiety within us because always there seems to be so little time for withdrawal, for reflection. These are the thoughts which find their way into our spirits when at last the Time of Quiet is our portion.

It is no ordinary experience to spread our lives before the honest scrutiny of our own selves, but there is no escape from such a necessity. The obvious things in our lives we pass over, taking them for granted; this may be a source of weakness and despair. Deeply are we aware of limitations in many dimensions of our lives. We are conscious of the ways in which and by which we have undermined the Light, the Truth, that is within; sometimes we do call good things bad and bad things good.

There are some things in our lives which we have not looked at for a long, long time. We make as an act of sacrament the lifting and exposing of these things before God, with tenderness and compassion. There are some things within us that are so far beneath the surface of our movements and our functioning that we are unmindful not only of their presence but also of the quality of their influence on our decisions, our judgment, and our behavior. In the quietness we will their exposure before God, that they may be lifted to the center of our focus, that we may know what they are and seek to deal with them in keeping with our health and our innermost wisdom.

All of the involvements of our lives in family, in primary community relations, in our state and country, and in the far-flung reaches of the things that we affect, and the things that affect us in our world; all of the concern that is ours for various aspects of the things that affect us and that we affect—these we spread before our own eyes and before the scrutiny of God.

123

We turn to Thee, Our Father, not out of a sense of worth or lack of worth, not out of a sense of pride or lack of pride, but we turn to Thee with our total life because this seems to speak directly to our deepest need. What Thou seest in us that is weak and unworthy of our best, wilt Thou handle in Thine own way. What Thou seest in us that is strong and vital, wilt Thou encompass in Thine own way. We yield as best we can, everything! everything! our Father, holding back nothing. We wait for Thy benediction and for Thy healing. We wait, O God, in the stillness of our own spirits. Amen.

90. The Season of Ingathering

THIS is the time of gathering in, the season of the harvest in nature. Many things that were started in the spring and early summer have grown to fruition and are now ready for reaping. Great and significant as is the harvest in nature, the most pertinent kind of ingathering for the human spirit is "the harvest of the heart." Long ago, Jesus said that men should not lay up for themselves treasures on earth, where moths corrupt and thieves break in and steal, but that men should lay up for themselves treasures in heaven. This insight suggests that life consists of planting and harvesting, of sowing and reaping. We are always in the midst of the harvest and always in the midst of the planting. The words that we use in communication, the profound stirrings of the mind out of which thoughts and ideas arise, the ebb and flow of desires out of which the simple or complex deed develops, are all caught in the process of reaping and sowing, of planting and harvesting. There are no anonymous deeds, no casual processes. Living is a shared process. Even as a man is conscious of things growing in him planted by others, which things are always ripening, so others are conscious of things growing in them planted by him, which things are always ripening. Inasmuch as he does not live or die unto himself, it is of the essence of wisdom for him conscientiously to live and die in the profound awareness of other people. "The statement 'Know thyself' has been taken mystically from the statement 'Thou hast seen thy brother, thou hast seen thy God.' "

91. The Quietness of This Waiting Moment

INTO the quietness of this Waiting Moment while our minds are filled with many of our personal and private involvements, may we seek together to center our thoughts and our feelings, our aspirations and our desires, to the end that as much of us as is possible may be available to the mind, to the wisdom, and to the love of God! Let us offer our lives, splintered as they are, fragmentary as they may be, let us offer our lives to Him.

Our experiences during the week that has passed move quietly before us. May we sift through them all until at last we find the most meaningful moment, the most searching experience that has come our way. We bring it into sharp focus before our minds and spirits: an act of sheer kindness which we received at the hands of a stranger or a casual acquaintance, the instructive response to some human need with which we were suddenly confronted; a harsh word spoken in anger, and now, no word of ours seems able to undo the damage wrought; a telephone call that opened up for us the inner reaches of another's heart, leaving us in breathless wonder.

We finger tenderly our hopes, our dreams, our fears, our anxieties. We spread our concerns in the quietness: the concerns which we have for our loved ones; the concerns which we have for the condition of the world; the riding threat of war and the smothered violences that choke the aspirations for peace and integrity among people whose lands are not their own, whose days are harassed by vast controls and subtle cruelties; the concern for justice and order in our land where injustice breeds hostilities and disorder threatens the very foundation of our simple securities.

We look with careful scrutiny at our responsibilities and weigh them against our freedom and our private plans: responsibility for those dependent upon us for bread and for hope; responsibility for commitments which we made when visions were clear and faith flowed freely through all our plans; responsibility for the day's work, the honest effort, and the true insight.

Our Father, we still ourselves deeply in Thy Presence, each with his own life's fact held surely there. Leave us not to the devices of our spirits or the cleverness of our minds, but shelter us with Thy love until we are cleansed and redeemed to be to ourselves and to Thee what makes Thee glad in us and in the way that we take. Amen.

92. The Light of His Spirit

IN MANY WAYS beyond all calculation and reflection, our lives have been deeply touched and influenced by the character, the teaching, and the spirit of Jesus of Nazareth. He moves in and out upon the horizon of our days like some fleeting ghost. At times, when we are least aware and least prepared, some startling clear thrust of his mind is our portion—the normal tempo of our ways is turned back upon itself and we are reminded of what we are, and of what life is. Often the judgment of such moments is swift and silencing: sometimes his insight kindles a wistful longing in the heart, softened by the muted cadence of unfulfilled dreams and unrealized hopes. Sometimes his words stir to life long forgotten resolutions, call to mind an earlier time when our feet were set in a good path and our plan was for holy endeavor. Like a great wind they move, fanning into flame the burning spirit of the living God, and our leaden spirits are given wings that sweep beyond all vistas and beyond all horizons.

There is no way to balance the debt we owe to the spirit which he let loose in the world. It is upon this that we meditate now in the gathering quietness. Each of us, in his own way, finds the stairs leading to the Holy Place. We gather in our hands the fragments of our lives, searching eagerly for some creative synthesis, some wholeness, some all-encompassing unity, capable of stilling the tempests within us and quieting all the inner turbulence of our fears. We seek to walk in our own path which opens up before us, made clear by the light of his spirit and the radiance which it casts all around us. We join him in the almighty trust that God is our Father and we are His children living under the shadow of His Spirit.

Accept the offering of our lives, O God; we do not know quite what to do with them. We place them before Thee as they are, encumbered and fragmented, with no hints, no suggestions, no attempts to order the working of Thy Spirit upon us. Accept our lives, our Father—work them over. Correct them. Purify them. Hold them in Thy focus lest we perish and the spirit within us dies. Amen.

93. The Littleness of Our Lives

IT IS a wonderfully blessed thing to be privileged to share together the common mood of worship. Miraculous indeed is it to mingle the individual life with its intensely private quality in a transcendent moment of sythesis and fusion—here it is that the uniquely personal is lifted up and seen in a perspective as broad as life, and as profound!

Again and again we are overwhelmed by the littleness of our lives. We are struck by the way in which there seems to close in upon us the intimate need, the demand that often provides no breathing moment sufficient to let us lift up our hearts to take the long look and to sense the utlimate meanings in which our little lives are involved. And yet for those of us who seek it out there is the time of respite and repair when we rest our lives in the Presence of God.

Our needs are so varied and poignant. There are some of us who are in the throes of great and bedeviling temptations which seem to know us by name and face us at the point of our greatest weakness and challenge us where there is no strength and no protection. For some of us anxiety is mounting within so that we are paralyzed by the thought of tomorrow and what awaits us in the coming day. In our desperation we are possessed by panic and are unable to face ourselves even in the Presence of God.

Always there are those of us who are ill in body. In vain we have tried to companion our pain to rob it of its power to eat away the grounds of our peace. If we could know the meaning of what besets us, or at least the effect that it may have upon the length of our days, this would be sustaining. We struggle with an undertone of uneasiness as we sift out the findings of the trained mind and the skilled hand.

We keep a troubled vigil at the bedside of the world. We cannot accept its sickness as unto death but we cannot grasp the meaning and the hope of a cure that will make life all about us hale and well. The contemplation of the destruction of the world at our hands confronts even our little lives and their little part with a guilt too vast to assuage and too overwhelming to manage.

Thus we clutch the moment of intimacy in worship when we become momentarily a part of a larger whole, a fleeting strength, which we pit against all the darkness and the dread of other times.

Our Father, we steady our lives before Thee in this waiting moment. Quicken our spirits with Thy Spirit that we may be "readied" anew for the living of our lives, whatever may be the particular circumstances of our tomorrows. Amen.

94. The Quiet Ministry of the Spirit

IT IS good to experience the quiet ministry of the living spirit of the living God. Again and again there are the little healings of silent breaches which sustain us in our contacts with the world and with one another. We are stunned by the little word, the unexpected silence, the smile off key; without quite knowing why, the balance is recovered and the rhythm of the hurt is stopped in its place. There is the sense of estrangement which overtakes the happiest human relations and the experience of recovery that makes the heart sing its old song with a new lilt. There are days when everything seems difficult, when the ordinary tasks become major undertakings, when one is sensitive and every moment is threatened by an explosion that does not quite come to pass; then without apparent cause, the whole picture changes and the spirit can breathe again with ease, the spring in the step comes back again. It is good to experience the quiet ministry of the living spirit of the living God.

Sometimes we are catapulted into disaster with a suddenness that paralyzes the mind and leaves the exposure to fear unshielded by courage or by strength. If there had been some warning, some intimation of what was to come, the wisdom of the years could have buttressed the life with a measured protection. But no, this was not the case. Often even before the full awareness of what has taken place can be felt, the realignment of one's powers begins to work and recovery is on the way. There are problems that meet us head-on in our journey. The issue of our spirit and the thing that confronts us is joined—we are engulfed in the great silence of fateful struggle. It seems that nowhere, in no place, can an answer be found. In vain we seek a clue, a key, even a little thing to give a fleeting respite, a second wind. Again and again it is apt to happen: the miracle of relief; a chance word from a casual conversation; a sentiment or a line in a letter; the refrain of an old song; an image from the past; a paragraph from a printed page; a stirring of prayer in the heart— the miracle of relief and we are released. The danger is passed, the conflict is over. It is good, so very good, to experience the quiet ministry of the living spirit of the living God.

We thank Thee, our Father, that Thou has not left us alone in the living of our lives. For us this is so, not because we are worthy or unworthy, because we are good or bad, but because we are Thy children. We rejoice that through all the vicissitudes of our lives Thou dost commune with Thyself through us and even the travail of our souls leaves us unafraid. Amen.

95. A Personal Presence Everywhere

"THE only strength for me is to be found in the sense of a personal presence everywhere. It scarcely matters whether it be called human or divine; a presence which only makes itself felt at first in this or that particular form and picture. . . . Into this presence we come, not by leaving behind what are usually called earthly things; or by loving them less, but by living more intensely in them, and loving more what is really lovable in them; for it is literally true that this world is everything to us, if only we choose to make it so, if only we 'live in the present' because it is eternity." Thus wrote Henry Nettleship toward the end of the nineteenth century.

In a very real sense we are earthbound creatures, caught always in the rigid context by which our experiences are defined. The particular fact or experience which we are facing at the moment, or the memory of other particular facts or experiences from other moments —these are our openings, these are the doors through which we enter into wider meanings, into wider contexts. When our little world of particular experiences seems to be illumined by more, much more, than itself, and we seem to be caught up into something bigger than our little lives, we give to such moments special names. They become watershed times. We mark the times in special ways, with special symbols. If it is the love of man and woman, it is the ring, the ceremonial, or the deep stillness of intimate disclosure; if it is the peak of joy, the emptying of the soul in suffering, or the fragmented activities of the daily round, there is the sense of Altar, the searching phrase from the holy book, or the gathered tear and the quickening pulse. At such times, and myriad others perhaps, we know that we live our way deeply in the present, only to discover that we are invaded by the Eternal.

Sensitize our spirits, our Father, that we may tread reverently in the common way, mindful that the glory of the Eternal is our companion. May we shrink not from the present intensity of our experiences lest we turn away from the redeeming power of Thy Perfect Love. Amen.

96. Your Loneliness

WHAT do you do with your loneliness? One of the massive results of the invasion of privacy so characteristic of our times is the increasing fear of being alone. Loneliness is of many kinds. There is the loneliness of a great bitterness when the pain is so great that any contact with others threatens to open old wounds and to awaken old frenzies. There is the loneliness of the broken heart and the dead friendship when what was full of promise and fulfillment lost its way in a fog of misunderstanding, anxiety, and fear. There is the loneliness of those who have absorbed so much of violence that all hurt has died, leaving only the charred reminder of a lost awareness. There is the loneliness of the shy and the retiring where timidity stands guard against all encounters and the will to relate to others is stilled. There is the loneliness of despair, the exhaustion of the spirit, leaving no strength to try again, the promise of the second wind can find no backing. There is the loneliness of death when silently a man listens, one by one, to the closing of all doors, and all that remains is naked life, stripped of everything that shields, protects, and insulates.

But there is loneliness in another key. There is the loneliness of the truth-seeker whose search swings him out beyond all frontiers and all boundaries until there bursts upon his view a fleeting moment of utter awareness and he *knows* beyond all doubt, all contradictions. There is the loneliness of the moment of integrity when the declaration of the self is demanded and the commitment gives no corner to sham, to pretense, or to lying. There is the loneliness in the moment of creation when the new comes into being, trembles, then steadies and finds its way. There is the loneliness of those who walk with God until the path takes them out beyond all creeds and all faiths and they know the wholeness of communion and the bliss of finally being understood.

Loneliness is of many kinds. What do you do with yours?

97. The Practice of His Presence

VARIED and rich are the methods used by individuals who have discovered the strength and the security that come from the practice of the Presence of God. Most often these practices are very private and are a part of the intimate resources of personal religious living. To talk about such things is like living one's private life in public. In the course of a lifetime a person may be privileged to share the testimony in most unexpected ways.

During the later years of her life, my mother spent a winter living in our home. Near the close of her visit I remarked on a particular Friday noon that she was not having lunch. She parried the comment, obviously throwing me off. This excited my curiosity, for it was unlike her not to be direct. After some moments of talking back and forth, it developed that it had been her habit for more than twenty years to fast every Friday, devoting as much time as possible to prayer and meditation. This had been going on for more than twenty years, and despite the fact that I had spent a part of each of those years with her, so undemonstrative had she been in her own private religious life that I was not aware of the fasting—had no hint of it. I was deeply puzzled—and am still puzzled!—as to how she had managed it.

There is a friend who is in her seventies now. In her professional life she was a secretary. Each morning before she has her breakfast she sits at her typewriter and writes a letter to God. No one else ever sees what she writes. It is part of her own private communion with Him.

There is another person well into the later years. For some months now she has been in uncertain health. Each morning when she awakes, she stops for a period of meditation. The phrase is the same each day: "This is the day the Lord has made. I will rejoice and be glad in it." At night, as she turns out the light over her bed, she says it a little differently because "rejoice" and "be glad" are not very restful words. She says, "This is the night which the Lord has made. I will rest and relax in it." One day she had a fall, but managed to pull herself up without calling for help. She was quite shaken and was in much pain. She prepared herself for bed and with much discomfort was able to get in beneath the covers. As she turned out the light, she said, "This is the night which the Lord has made. I will relax and cry in it." Then she realized what she had said, and her tears were all mixed with her laughter.

Varied and rich indeed are the methods used by individuals who have discovered the strength and serenity that come from the "practice of the Presence of God." What have you found needful for your peace?

98. Our Spirits Remember God

It is good to remember that God has not left Himself without a witness in our spirits. There is a Spirit in us that contains our spirit, that provides the secondary consolations which float the big anxieties, that sustains the effort beyond the calculated endurance, that makes the case for the good impulse when the rational judgment sends the mind spinning in the opposite way, that brooks over all weariness and all despair until the change comes and the heart is revived, that holds the confidence in the integrity of the self when the deeds that contradict will not be stilled and the act that destroys goes on its relentless way—it is good to remember the God has not left Himself without a witness in our spirits.

It is good to remember that God has not left Himself without a witness in our lives. There is at work in life much that seems so circumstantial that the release of explanation can come only by the great word of the noncommittal: coincidence. Even the most cursory examination of what may be regarded as the most commonplace life, shows that at many points startling things have occurred that altered the entire direction of the life: some chance word heard at a critical moment, some single encounter along the way, a paragraph tucked away in an ordinary book, a stray thought out of nowhere, finds a cuddling place in the mind and there begins to live and breathe and reproduce its kind until something emerges as a new outlook, a different way of thinking. It is good to remember that God has not left Himself without a witness in our lives.

Despite all the wanderings of our footsteps, despite all the ways by which we may have sought to circumvent the truth within us, despite all the weaknesses of spirit and of mind, despite all the blunders by which we may have isolated ourselves from our fellows or proven unworthy of the love, the trust, the confidence, by which again and again our faltering lives are surrounded, despite all these things it is good to remember that God has not left Himself without a witness in our spirits and in our lives.

99. The Critical Option

IN ONE of Fénelon's reflections he writes: "What wilt thou have me to do? I am ready to do everything and to do nothing, to desire nothing and to desire everything, to suffer without consolation, and to take comfort in the sweetest consolations. I do not say to thee, 'O God, I will perform the most difficult acts of self-denial, I will make striking changes in my conduct.' It is not for me to decide what I will do. What I will do is to listen to thee, and to await the dictates of thy Law."

The quality of life is often determined by that to which the individual is dedicated. If the dedication of the life is vague and diffuse, the quality is apt to be poor and weak. There is much to be said for the intensity of life focus which structures and defines where the individual places the living emphasis of his days. It may be that there has been developed no particular vocational emphasis in the life; it may be that one merely has a job that provides food, shelter, and a modicum of personal security. It may be that there can be no change in such a situation for the duration of the life. Under such circumstances it is easy to accept life as being without point and purpose. One waits in vain for some great challenge to lift one out of the weary rut that slowly deepens and finally engulfs. "If something could happen to me," "If I had something to look forward to, all life would be different; but for me there is nothing and there never has been anything— ever since I can remember"—these are the outbursts of many persons.

Fénelon puts his finger on an important clue. Granted that the daily round is monotonous, that the personal equipment is extremely limited, that all the options were frozen long ago, that there is no thing on the horizon that sounds the trumpet call to the great adventure or the high demand—granted all of this. But there is always available to the individual another alternative even where options are frozen. One can make an offering of the self to God. This is far different from offering one's special talents, as important as that may be. It is more than the offering of resources, however great or limited they may be. It is to offer one's self: to put at the disposal of

Life one's life, not merely one's needs, one's demands, one's frustrations, one's unresolved problems. This is to say to Life, "Here I am, I put myself at your disposal to be where I am—all of me. To do, where I am, with all of me. To respond to life where I am without bargaining or bartering." This means more than being a dutiful son or satisfied worker in a monotonous job. It means putting one's self at the disposal of the hours, of the days, of the months, to feel of their quality, to sense their demands independent of what one demands, independent of what one thinks should come back in dividends. With this freedom of movement within one's own spirit provision is made for the meaningful activity and the significant undertaking—all of this without any apparent change in one's external circumstances.

"What wilt thou have me do? I am ready to do everything and to do nothing, to desire nothing and to desire everything."

100. The Many Selves Become One

IN THY Presence we become aware of many divisions within the inner circle of the Self. When we enter into communion with Thee, we are never sure of the Voice that speaks within us. We do not always know which voice is the true Voice.

Sometimes it is the clear call of the heart remembering an unfulfilled hunger from other days; sometimes it is but an echo of some "failing impulse to good" which we have pushed aside that a private end may triumph even in the face of the distinct call of truth; often it is the muttering of needs that do not shape themselves in words because they are one with all the ebb and flow of every passing day; at times the Voice is like a clarion rising above all conflicts and confusion, so uttering the need for courage to stand against some evil, to witness for the good where the cost is high and the penalty great; sometimes the Voice is muted, telling of hopes unrealized and dreams that will not rest until they incarnate themselves in us—all the while we pull back but they will not let us go.

In the midst of all the sounds rising above all the mingled words there is a strange Voice—but not quite a stranger. A man recognizes it. It seems to come from every part of him but cannot rest itself on any point of sound. He waits. He listens. When all is still, he listens now at a deeper level of silence. In soundless movement there floats up through all the chambers of his being, encompassing all the tongued cries from many selves, one word: God—God—God. And the answer is the same, filling all the living silence before Thy Face: God—God—God.

101. The Waiting Moment

THE news on every hand and from every land carries tidings of disturbance and impending disaster!

Sometimes the story tells of a wild moment when all the saneness of earth and sky departs, leaving a churning residue of mindless violence; of floods that empty the land of goodness, earthquakes that give birth to vast shambles, pestilence that lays waste tissue and blood, hunger that grips and chokes the life of young and old alike, fears that ride herd to all confidence and hope, despair that turns to ashes every dream that would quicken the heart.

Of all these we are profoundly mindful as we find ourselves in the stillness of the Waiting Moment.

But these do not complete the list, our Father. Within ourselves we find the living fiber of much of which the tidings tell. The intimate awareness of our private poverty closes in upon us. We would love but are not skilled in the art. We would give but we do not know to what or to whom. We would seek Thee but there is so little heart in our quest. We would triumph over our weaknesses but the zeal ever escapes us. We would honor the light within but there is so much comfort in the darkness. We would pray but our spirits cannot even focus on our needs; the intimate awareness of our private poverty closes in upon us.

This is not all, thank God! There is a spirit within and about us that broods over every tiding, encircling all our needs. It breathes through the Waiting Moment, cradling all that is. We thank Thee, our Father, for such a Witness of Thyself. Let us into the awareness of Thy deep intent that we may know Thy purpose in the human story and in the private way. We would not be turned aside from Thee by all the evil tidings, by all the wasteland of our spirits. Often it is so hard to find Thee—find Thee we must. Hold us steady in Thy grace that we may be found of Thee. How blessed, O God, is the ingathering of the Waiting Moment!

102. The Twofold Encounter

THE individual has a twofold encounter with the God of the universe. In one dimension of the encounter the individual seeks to lay bare the totality of his life before God. There is intimate confession of sin against God; the quiet and sometimes turbulent awareness that the life of man is lived under the awful scrutiny of God. At such a moment the integrity of the deed and of the person is placed upon the altar to be purified and purged by ultimate judgment and forgiveness. All pretenses are swept away and out of the depths of the soul rises the cry of atonement. Here is a universal necessity enthroned in the formal worship as embodied in a great and particular religious faith and tradition. The nation or the individual who undertakes to live without the winnowing vitality of the Day of Reckoning has no point of ultimate referral to inform his days and to structure his life. The fruit of that kind of living is bitter and full of death. God deliver our nation from such a disaster.

But there is another dimension of the encounter. It is at the level of brotherhood and community with the children of God. This encounter is instinct with the demand that all broken harmonies with our fellows be repaired and restored. Wherever there is estrangement, there must be reconciliation. Wounds must be healed, crooked paths made straight, and the turbulence of human conflict subdued by the tranquillity of forgiveness and the will to community. Hatreds upon which life has fed must be uprooted by great contrition and the felt necessity for forgiveness.

These are the two dimensions of the encounter. A man dare not face his God on the Day of Atonement, seeking a right relation with Him, unless he has already exhausted himself in redeeming all the broken relations that he has with his fellows. There is an august impertinence and an utter arrogance in coming before God seeking for one's self at His hands what one has refused to give to those who walk the common way from day to day.

"Forgive us our debts as we forgive our debtors": this is the timeless utterance, the password that relaxes the Angel with the Flaming Sword who guards the entrance to the Holy of Holies. No man can be happy in Heaven if *he* left his brother in Hell.

Psalm 139

Search me and know my heart.

103. Thou Hast Searched Me and Known Me

IN ALL places
  Where I have dallied in joyous abandon,
  Where I have responded to ancient desires and yielded
    to impulses old as life, blinded like things that move
    without sight;
  Where chores have remained chores, unfulfilled by
    laziness of spirit and sluggishness of mind;
  Where work has been stripped of joy by the ruthless
    pruning of vagrant ambition;
  Where the task has been betrayed by slovenly effort;
  Where the response to human need has been halfhearted
    and weak;
  Where the surge of strength has spent itself in great
    concentration and I have been left a shaking reed in
    the wind;
  Where hope has mounted until from its quivering height
    I have seen the glory and wonder of the new dawn
    of great awakening;
  Where the quiet hush of utter surrender envelops me
    in the great silence of intimate commitment;
Thou hast known me!

  When I have lost my way, and thick fog has shrouded
    from my view the familiar path and the lights of home;
  When with deliberate intent I have turned my back on
    truth and peace;
  When in the midst of the crowd I have sought refuge
    among the strangers;

When things to do have peopled my days with mounting
    anxiety and ever-deepening frustration;
When in loneliness I have sat in the thicket of despair
    too weak to move, to lift my head;
Thou hast searched for and found me!

I cannot escape Thy Scrutiny!
I would not escape Thy Love!

104. Thou Art Acquainted with All My Ways

WITH all my ways,
Thou art acquainted:
    The silent coming together of all the streams
    Nourished by springs of Being
    Fountained in ancient sires
    Since Life began:
        The quiet shaping of patterns,
        That gave meaning and substance
        To all I know as mine:
            The nurture of mother,
            The molding of climate,
            The rending of heritage
            That stamped their mark in tender mind
                and growing limb;
            The tutoring by playmates
                and those who instruct;
            The sure hand of Spirit
                that held in keeping
                sensitive meanings of right and wrong . . .

With all my ways
Thou art acquainted:
    The making of plans far below the level

of the daily mind
that find their way to guide
the movement of the deed—
Habits that monitor the freshness
in all spontaneity
and tame the glory of the creative act;
The unrestrained joy of impulse
sweeping all before it in riotous rejoicing;
The great tenderness called to life
by that which invades the heart
and circles all desires;
The little malices;
The big hostilities;
The subtle envies;
The robust greeds;
The whimpering contrition;
The great confession;
The single resolve;
The fearful commitment;
The tryst with Death
that broods over the zest for life
like intermittent shadows
from sunrise to sunset—

Thou art acquainted—
Thou art acquainted—
With all my ways.

105. Thou Hast Beset Me Behind and Before

THOU hast beset me behind and before
And laid Thine hand upon me!

The upward push of life awakes the egg,
an inner stirring sends it forth
to be in all its parts according to its law.

The blossom opens wide its heart
to wind and bee,
then closes.
Deep within its pulsing core
the dream of fruit takes shape
and life decrees what it must be!
The little chick mingles sound with
baby duck and goose,
sharing each the common food,
drinking from the single trough;
Day after day breezes blow—
Rains bring to one and all the glad
refreshment from the summer's sun—
Yet, each follows his appointed way,
without an awkward turn;
Each fulfills the pattern of his own design.
From tiny cell or ripened fruit,
From baby chick or mammoth oak
the same refrain goes forth:

Thou hast beset me behind and before
And laid Thine hand upon me!

Muscle by muscle,
Bone by bone,
Adding to strength and height,
This the journey from infancy to youth;
Growing by day, by night;
Growth makes an end.
Some order calls a halt!
Beset behind, before,
Growth gives way.
But life does not stop,
The twins keep pace:
Joy, sorrow—
Sickness, health—
Success, failure—

Hope, despair—
Courage, fear—
Peace, turmoil.
The tempo quickens:
Dreams long cherished fall apart;
Slumbering desires awaken in vital strength;
The good seems no longer good;
The evil allures and engulfs;
The will is weak, the path grows dim,
Doubts gather, confusion is confounded,
Endurance languishes,
The spirit holds—
Till life begins anew.

Thou hast beset me behind and before
And laid Thine hand upon me!

106. Thou Knowest It Altogether

MY WORDS cry out to give their hearts away:
Each has its story and comes from afar.
Again and again I seek my way with them,
To ring them round with well-kept secrets
Known to me, to me alone.

Sometimes they are willing carriers of private ends
Spending their strength in missions not their own.
Sometimes they rebel against the quality of my need
And force their way into another's heart,
Betraying the secrets I would not share.
Sometimes the full sweep of urgency
Frightens all speech,
Leaving me bruised and shaken.

My words cry out to give their hearts away:
The integrity of the word—

Where may it be found?
Is it meanings the word has gained from all
   its wanderings through the wilderness of sounds
   in many lands, in far-off places?
Is it the self-offering of the word to the honest
   seeker after truth
   that it may blend its secret with the deep resolve?
Is it something outside the word—
   some meaning a man would share beyond the word itself?
Is there only the integrity of the man?

To domesticate the word;
To safeguard its character;
To purge the violence from its face;
To allow no service that defiles, degrades;
To make it one with truth;
To fill it with the pure intent;
This is to make the word the Sacrament,
The Angelos of God.
This is the breath of life that makes man, man.
   For there is not a word in my tongue
   But lo, Thou knowest it altogether.

107. Whither Shall I Go from Thy Presence

WHITHER shall I go from Thy Presence?
From Thee is there some hiding place?

   The deed is a thing so private,
   So inside the perfect working of desire
   That its inward part seems known to me,
   To me alone.

   The ebb and flow of thoughts
   Within my hidden sea,

The forms that stir within the channels of my mind,
Keep tryst with all my hidden hopes and fears.

The ties that hold me fast to those
Whose life with mine makes one,
The tangled twine that binds my life
With things I claim as mine,
Are held in place by folds
Of my embrace.

The sealéd stillness that walls around
The heartaches and the pain,
Is held against all else that would invade.

Awe-filled contrition emptied clear
Of violence and sin,
Seeps slowly from the wilderness
Of my deserted soul.

Almighty joy mounts to the brim
And overflows in wild array,
With music only ears attuned can hear.

And yet,
Always I know that Another
Sees and understands—
Every vigil with me keeps watch—
The door through which He comes no man
Can shut—
He is the Door!

I cannot go from Thy Presence,
There is no hiding place from Thee.

108. If I Ascend up into Heaven, Thou Art There!

IF I ascend up into heaven, Thou art there!
    When my joy overflows and
    No words contain it;
    When the thing I sought was lost
    Only to reappear within the hollow of my hand;
    When the day seems interminable
    But at eventide the burdens lift
    And weariness is a far-off memory;
    When there opens before the vista of the mind
    The wonder of new regions, far-off places;
    When the gentle touch of a loved one
    Makes music heard only by the listening heart;
    When the doctor's word is the final word
    And deep within the hidden places of the life
    Healing waters stir, bringing wholeness in their wake—
    When the wanderer comes home
    And the wayward finds peace in the ancient fireside—
    When from the ashes of old dreams
    The fires of a new life are kindled—
    Thou art there!

If I make my bed in hell—behold—

    When night remains night
    And darkness deepens;
    When the evilness of evil is unrelieved
    And utter desolation makes mockery
    Of all that was true and good;
    When the open door of refuge
    Closes in my face
    And to turn back is of no avail;
    When the firm grip of sanity trembles
    And all balances tilt, leaving

The mind tortured and crazed;
When all around, worlds crash
And winds blow torrid
Over the parched and wasted
Places of my spirit;
When sin multiplies itself
Until at last all goodness
Seems swallowed up and devoured;
When the chuckle of death
Is the only sound to be heard in the land,
Thou art there!

If I make my bed in hell . . .
If I ascend up into heaven . . .
   Behold!

109. In Thy Book All My Members Are Written

THE organism! How rare a thing it is!

The miracle of Hand:
   Fingers and thumbs
   Caught up in single grasp,
   Holding, shaping, fashioning outward things,
   To make the dream a fact.
The miracle of Parts:
   A restless muscle sending blood day unto day
   To sustain the rhythm of lungs, in and out,
   To keep alive the cell and striding step;
   The measured growth of bone
   To make the wholesome balance, the upright stance;
   Great network of nerves reaching everywhere
   To alert, to caution,
   To gather news on every hand
   To keep the world in place,
   That meaning may remain;

The vital brain
The Watchman on the Wall
Controlling, dispatching,
Interpreting, deciding,
Holding within its tiny folds,
The private journey and the grooved way . . .
The miracle of Mind:
Everywhere felt,
Nowhere seen;
A thing, no thing;
Matter, no matter;
Fleeting in passage,
Ever unmoving;
The Master of the House,
The Servant of All;
Reflection and image
All in one!

Great God! How vast must be Thy Faith
To risk so much in such a tiny frame;
To bring to being and to teach to praise
A living threat to all Thy nourished dreams!
And yet, not so—
Upon each part, the holy stamp:
"In Thy Book all my members are written
which in continuance were fashioned
when as yet, there was none of them!"

110. How Precious Are Thy Thoughts Unto Me, O God!

How precious are Thy thoughts!

The nerve of life abounds in all I see,
The kernel of the seed holds in its place a swinging door,
Through which the boundless energy of living substance flows,
Forming itself in root and stalk, in branch and fruit.

The germ in the egg awaits
The pregnant moment:
A gentle tug, a brooding urge,
An unhurried push to full creation,
Then living form of chick, or bird, or child.

A whisper in the mind—
A voice floating in the hills
Calling to itself
Kindred thoughts from far-off places;
Ideas take shape and form,
Firming within their vital wall,
A strange insistence:
They pull, they push, they drive,
Command!
Until, at last, they are
The Master in the House;
And the whole course of man's life
Is channeled into regions he does not know,
Nor scarcely understands.

How precious are Thy thoughts!

The response to goodness, the urge to minister;
The quickened willingness to bless;
The deep rejection of the evil deed, revealed;
The pull of the clear thought, the honest desire;
An all-embracing tenderness cradling the kindly act;
The far-flung hope comprising myriad strands of all man's
   dreams;
The hard rebuff to all that mocks and scorns;
The whole surrender of the center of consent,
To lose life only to find it again.

How precious are Thy thoughts unto me, O God!
How great is the sum of them!

111. When I Awake, I Am Still with Thee

IN ALL the waking hours
The Tentacles of Time
Give channel to each living thing:
   The bird on wing;
   The mole moving in darkness underground;
   The cricket chanting its evening song;
   The primeval whale sporting in chilly seas,
      or floating noiselessly in turbulent waters;
   In mountain crevice or sprawling meadow
   The delicate beauty of color-stained flower
      or fragile leaf;
   High above the timber line
      The sprig of green dares wind and snow;
   In the barren parchness of desert waste
      The juiceless shrub and waterlogged cactus;
   High in the treetop the green-pearled fruit
      of olive mistletoe,
        and the soft gray stillness of creeping moss;
   The infant, the growing child,
   The stumbling adolescent, the young adult,
   The man full blown or stooped with years;
   The Tentacles of Time
   Give channel to each living thing.

And beyond this?
   Thoughts that move with grace of being:
   Light thoughts that dance and sing
   Untouched by gloom or shadow or the dark;
   Weighty thoughts that press upon the road
      with tracks that blossom into dreams
      or shape themselves in plan and scheme;
   Thoughts that whisper;

Thoughts that shout;
Thoughts that wander without rest,
   Seeking, seeking, always seeking;
Thoughts that challenge;
Thoughts that soothe;
The Tentacles of Time
Give channel to each living thing.

Out from the House of Life
All things come,
And into it, each returns again for rest.

When I awake,
I am still with Thee.

112. I Hate Them with Perfect Hate

THERE is a weary joy in all revenge!
When a man's rejoicing
Over the broken lances of his vanquished foe
Leaves him clean and fresh and free.
   Or so it seems.
   It matters not, the violence—
   The bitterness spewed out of his hating heart . .
   Is there no law?
   The sowing and reaping—
   Are they ever one?
Can man escape the consequence?
Can it ever be true?
   The enemy caught in my vital wrath—
   Was he not reaping what was sown?
   The penalty of my revenge,
   Was it but the operation of law?
   He had piled deed upon deed upon deed,
   Reckless of all returns;
   Emptied each hour of all the good,

Ringing it round with deeds that hurt,
With things that kill.
Is that not so?
In what he did
Was he not enemy of good,
Of God?
In my response, was I but a living thing
In Holy Hands—
Carrying out the law
Of which I am a part?
My hatred then is perfect
And I am free of stain.
But am I?
The vengeance which I execute
Becomes fresh seeds of violence sown,
And I must reap;
Or all is void.
It matters not the cause—
The consequence remains.

"Vengeance is mine," saith the Lord,
"I will repay."

I rest my soul at last in this
And find my peace.

113. Try Me and Know My Thoughts

JUDGMENT seems far removed from act and deed.
Trumpets from the Past sound warning notes:
   The Day of Judgment!
   Prepare to meet thy God!
Beyond the gates of modern life
Ancient myths couched in dogmas old
Mold and rot in silent gloom:
   The end of time,

God on His Throne to judge mankind,
And a man alone stands before
The Judgment Seat;
The sky, a canopy above,
Heavenly floats:
> Angels, archangels, in ceaseless flight
> Bathed in Eternal Light forever,
> Blazing forth from the Throne of God . . .
> Such is the ancient myth.

Now man is free
To live unmindful of impending doom;
> Or so it seems.
There is a timeless warning in the far-off word,
The bitter truth returns in many forms;
No deed, no act, stands by itself alone.
> In bone and blood,
> In nerve and cell,
> In all the imagery of mind,
> In sound of voice,
> In wrinkled brow,
> Standing, sitting,
> Waking, sleeping,
> Laughter, tears,
> Imprint of thought,
> Registry of deed
> Remain for all man's days.
> There is a tight circle
> In which man moves.
> Nothing escapes;
> Soon or late,
> Somewhere, somewhen,
> The doer and the deed
> Are face to face!
The ancient myth renews its truth:
And a man stands alone

Before the Judgment Seat!
Try me, O God, and know my thoughts

And see if there be any wicked way
Within me!